POE T'S

BOOK-SHELF

Contemporary

Poets On Books

That Shaped

Their Art

Edited by Peter Davis

ISBN: 0-935306-50-1

ACKNOWLEDGEMENTS

The editor and publisher are grateful to the poets who, so graciously, contributed entries and encouragement, and to the many friends, colleagues, and students who helped with the publication of this book, especially Jen Davis, Nancy Green-Madia, Alex and Lucas Perry, Nina B. Marshall, Mark Neely, and Thom Tammaro.

"The afterthought." By Cid Corman, from SUN ROCK MAN, copyright © 1970 by Cid Corman. Reprinted by permission of New Directions Publishing Corp.

"A Litany for Survival," from THE BLACK UNICORN by Audre Lorde. Copyright © 1978 by Audre Lorde. Used by permission of W. W. Norton & Company, Inc.

"At Night," translated by Tania and James Stern, from FRANZ KAFKA: THE COMPLETE STORIES by Franz Kafka, edited by Nahum N. Glatzer, copyright 1946, 1947, 1948, 1949, 1954, 1958, 1971 by Schocken Books. Used by permission of Schocken Books, a division of Random House, Inc.

"Dutch Interior": From VALENTINE PLACE by David Lehman (Scribner, 1996). Copyright © 1996 by David Lehman; reprinted by permission of the author.

Acknowledgements continue on page 221.

The Barnwood Press (barnwoodpress.org)
PO Box 146
Selma IN 47383

Printed by Consolidated Printing, Farmland, Indiana.

for my dad

CONTENTS

PREFACE

When I was studying for my MFA I was required to read 25 books, of my choosing, per semester. Once, I asked one of my professors to give me some suggestions and she gave me a list of 30 or so writers that she thought I should read. I didn't know if these were writers that were personally important to her, or if they were simply writers she thought might become important to me, but either way, I thought it was a great list. Soon after, I got the idea for this book and began asking leading contemporary poets to respond to these prompts:

    1) Please list 5-10 books that have been most "essential"
       to you, as a poet.
    2) Please write some comments about your list. You may
       want to single out specific poems or passages from the
       books, discuss how you made your decisions, or provide
       thoughts about the importance of these books in your life.
       Feel free to write as much as you would like.

I mentioned that the primary audience for the book might be younger poets, but that I believed many people would be interested. I asked a variety of poets because I wanted to represent a wide range of contemporary poetry.

I didn't know if anyone would respond. I figured, at the very worst, I'd end up with a few interesting lists and no book. To my relief and great happiness, 81 poets responded. Others sent notes of support, but didn't contribute for a variety of reasons: some didn't feel they could narrow their "essentials" into such a list, some were too busy, some had health problems, etc.

It was great to get each and every response. I was happy for the one sentence that Elizabeth Spires sent and the twelve pages that Clayton Eshleman sent. I was happy to get Charles Bernstein's response of four lists, containing thirteen titles each, and the response of Russell Edson who hesitated to list even one book. Some poets, in thoughtful and curious ways, didn't really address the prompts. Others reworded them. When it made sense (and it often did), I edited the responses to fit into the simple format of list, followed by comments. But, occasionally, even this didn't seem appropriate.

After compiling the responses, it seemed natural to wonder about who was listed most; and so, at the end of this book, I've included a list of "The Most Frequently Listed Authors." This list is not intended to offer a ranking of poets, or some kind of cannon. It's only purpose is to quickly satisfy curiosity about what was most frequently mentioned within the confines of this book.

I think I'm like most readers in that I discover good books mainly through one of two ways: either I get lucky and stumble across something I love, or I trust the word of someone–a friend, reviewer, teacher. When I began this book, I thought that it might help with both ways. I think it does.

There is much good, weird luck to be found here due to the variety of poets and the variety of books they mention. And, all things considered, who better to trust?

POET'S BOOKSHELF

AI

Fyodor Dostoevsky, *The Brothers Karamazov*
Richard Wright, *Native Son*
Galway Kinnell, *Body Rags*
James Wright, *Shall We Gather at the River*
W. S. Merwin, *The Lice*
William Faulkner, *As I Lay Dying*
Flannery O'Connor, *A Good Man Is Hard to Find*
Gabriel García Márquez, *One Hundred Years of Solitude*
Carlos Fuentes, *Where the Air Is Clear*
N. Scott Momaday, *House Made of Dawn*

I was a voracious reader from about the third grade on. During my senior year of high school, I began to form a rather dark view of the world after reading *The Brothers Karamazov* and *Native Son*. I preferred the romantic poets. In my junior year of college, I discovered the Beats, but, as I was a Japanese major, I was also reading Mishima, Kawabata and other fine Japanese fiction writers. I relaxed by reading science fiction. That junior year of college, when I took poetry work-shops, I began to read more poetry.

Although I thought Plath's poems were very fine, I found them somewhat cold and distanced, but I loved and was very moved by Galway Kinnell's *Body Rags*. I also respected and was greatly moved by *Shall We Gather at the River*, by James Wright and *The Lice*, by W. S. Merwin. My appreciation of Kinnell's book was enhanced by the fact that he came to read at the University of Arizona, where I was a student. Because those poets were presented to me by my teacher, Richard Shelton, as poets to be inspired by, I was open to what they had to say in their work and, also, because they were alive (I mean writing "now") I felt somewhat closer to them than to some of the other great poets we read. I must emphasize that I had a list of one hundred poets given to me by Shelton and I just read everything on the list, so my education in the fine art of writing poetry was not limited to the three I've chosen to mention, but I found them the most inspiring at the time.

After grad school, I was inspired by Faulkner's *As I Lay Dying* and Flannery O'Connor, especially *A Good Man Is Hard to Find*. To me, the Southern writers seemed to be able to lay bare the most hidden and distressing things about people, yet so skillfully, and with such abandon, that I very much enjoyed reading them.

At that time, I also began to read the Latin American and South

American writers. The first thing I read was *One Hundred Years of Solitude*, which, in a roundabout way, led to *Where the Air Is Clear.* Anyway, what can I say about *One Hundred Years of Solitude* that hasn't been said already? I also found Pedro Paramo very powerful and more like something I would write.

N. Scott Momaday's *House Made of Dawn* was the first fiction I read by a Native American. I identified with the main character's struggles. Anyway, I was just learning then, you know? Everything was new and exciting to me. In a way, I found everything I read inspiring.

NIN ANDREWS

Rainer Maria Rilke, *The Selected Poetry and Prose*, ed. Stephen
    Mitchell
Federico García Lorca, *The Selected Poems*, ed. Francisco García
    Lorca and David Allen
Yannis Ritsos, *Gestures*, trans. Nikos Stangos
Henri Michaux, *Selected Writings*, trans. Richard Ellman
Nina Cassian, *Life Sentences*

Every day for the past two weeks, I have tried to pick five or ten
books that are essential to me. Usually the choices would be simple.
Witty and acerbic poets are my favorites: Charles Bukowski, Henri
Michaux, Mark Halliday, Amy Gerstler, Tim Seibles. The Adams and
Eves of the avant garde, Houdinis of the heart, hymn singers of the humdrum.
I like to quote poems such as "Strawberry Milkshake" by Halliday or
"Dear Boy George" by Gerstler. Or this one from Henri Michaux:

Simplicity

What has been particularly lacking in my life up to
now is simplicity. Little by little I am beginning to change.

For example, I always go out with my bed now and
when a woman pleases me, I take her and go to bed
with her immediately.

If her ears are ugly and large, or her nose, I remove
them along with her clothes and put them under the
bed, for her to take back when she leaves; I keep only
what I like.

If her underthings would improve by being changed, I
change them immediately. That is my gift. But, if I see
a better-looking woman go by, I apologize to the first
and make her disappear at once.

People who know me claim that I am incapable of
doing what I just described, that I haven't enough
spunk. I once thought so myself, but that was because I
wasn't doing everything *just as I pleased*.

Now, I always have excellent afternoons. (Mornings I work.)

Ordinarily I'd want to discuss the appeal of the comic poet and try to explicate the logic of humor. On my wall I have posted this quote from the philosopher Henry Bergson: "You will find that the art of the comic poet consists in making us well acquainted with the particular vice, in introducing us, the spectators, to such a degree of intimacy with it, that in the end we get hold of some of the strings of the marionette with which he is playing, and actually work them ourselves; this explains some of the pleasure we feel."

But these days I'm not sure how anything works, and nothing seems particularly funny. I think of Camus, his belief that men are forever trying to convince themselves that they aren't absurd. Or Eugene O'Neill's statement: "Life is best regarded as a bad dream between two awakenings." Maybe it's the weather, gray skies day after day, an Ohio winter setting on so fast. Or the news, President Bush on the radio, sounding like a cross between a football coach and an evangelical Christian, the rumble of patriotism and war-fever, everyone driving by with red, white, and blue waving in the wind. I find myself humming "Onward Christian Soldiers" and wondering what country or century I am living in. Maybe as a result, I've been re-reading poetry books I haven't touched for years. Is this because these poets are more "essential"? I'm not sure.

Joseph Joubert writes, "Everything has its poetry." Joubert also writes, "In every piece of music, not everything is music, and in every poem, not everything is poetry." But what is the music of music, the poetry in a poem? What is the essential within the essential? I change my mind constantly. Maybe everything depends on the hour and its whims. The landscape inside out, or outside in. Like an Ashbery epiphany.

Poetry speaks so many languages. I sometimes think of them as the languages of heaven, purgatory, and hell. These days I am in any or all of these places. My father used to tell a story, how once he was driving down the highway in one state, staring out at the ocean, when suddenly he found himself in another state, the cornfields outside his window, the hot wind in his face. No time had passed, he had just moved, seamlessly, to his destination. No, he wasn't on drugs. Sometimes, he explained, what can't be is. I believed him then, and I believe him now. One day I am reading Rimbaud, "At dawn, / armed with burning patience / we shall enter / the splendid cities," and the next, I hear James Tate: "At dawn I would nudge you / with anxious fingers and say / Already we are in Idaho."

Lately, I've been wishing to escape from planet earth altogether. I've been overindulging in Rilke's angels, Rimbaud's splendid cities, Lorca's moons...poems such as Rilke's "Lament," and Lorca's "The Moon Rising." I am in the mood for romantic excess, the play of moonlight against the shadows of suffering, solemn trains of thought that follow me down the aisles of K-Mart or Staples and out into the wet streets. Like Baroque music or recipes for summer or some divine or ethereal tryst...Like a drug, a single drop of which transforms all the white spaces inside and changes everything: the curve and length of an hour, how it rests on the skin as a warm glow or vanishes without a trace or leaves a mark I can't erase...Or like the old model or maps of the world, back when people could drop off its edges and sail clear out of here...These poems make me feel as if I am sailing clear out of here.

I still remember the first time I was swept away by a poem. I was thirteen, working in a bookstore after school, still wearing my kilt and knee socks, when I flipped open Yannis Ritsos' book, *Gestures*, to the mystical little poem, "The Third One":

> The three of them sat before the window looking at the sea.
> One talked about the sea. The second listened. The third
> neither spoke nor listened; he was deep in the sea; he floated.
> Behind the windowpanes, his movements were slow, clear
> in the thin pale blue. He was exploring a sunken ship.
> He rang the dead bell for the watch; fine bubbles
> rose bursting with a soft sound-suddenly,
> "Did he drown?" asked one; the other said, "He drowned." The third one
> looked back at them helpless from the bottom of the sea, the
> way one looks at drowned people.

I felt then as I feel now when I read Ritsos, as if I were holding my breath, listening and looking through a keyhole at another world, which is in fact this one, only suddenly lit, more beautiful, and terrifying...Which reminds me of Rilke's lines: "For beauty is only the beginning of Terror, which we are still just able to endure." Often it's the simplest images of Ritsos that amaze and delight, images of a seamstress with a mouth full of pins, a woman gathering oranges while "I" gather the sun, and of "a stiff brown overcoat had taken on the shape of someone sleeping, pretending to be the one that had left."

I love the magical yet simple language and imagery, the fairy tale logic, the mystical visions and peculiar proclamations..."Did he drown?" Yes, of course he drowned. What else could he do if he were too deep in the world or sea? Yet there is something reassuring in the poet's ability to make despair and absurdity beautiful. In Lorca's poem, "The Moon Rising," he even prescribes a proper diet for one whose "heart feels like an island in infinity."

The Moon Rising

When the moon rises,
the bells hang silent,
and impenetrable footpaths
appear.

When the moon rises,
the sea covers the land,
and the heart feels
like an island in infinity.

Nobody eats oranges
under the full moon.
One must eat fruit
that is green and cold.

But the poet who overwhelms me entirely with angst and longing is Nina Cassian, whose poems bear titles such as "Romance," "Longing," "Greed," and "Kisses." In her poem, "Licentiousness," Cassian writes of: "the clitoris in my throat / vibrating, sensitive, pulsating / exploding in the orgasm of Romanian." I wonder if anyone could survive a desire this strong:

Temptation

Call yourself alive? Look, I promise you
that for the first time you'll feel your pores opening
like fish mouths, and you'll actually be able to hear
your blood surging through all those lanes,
and you'll feel light gliding across the cornea
like the train of a dress. For the first time
you'll be aware of gravity
like a thorn in your heel,
and your shoulder blades will ache for want of wings.
Call yourself alive? I promise you
you'll be deafened by the sound of dust falling on furniture,
you'll feel your eyebrows turning to two gashes,
and every memory you have–will begin
at Genesis.

Of course a person can read too many poems of beauty, Eros, and angels. After a while, one might feel almost Dido-esque. Then it's time to stop reading, push aside the books and simply listen. Be alone with the mind. Stare out the window or watch the air growing lighter or darker. There is a kind of intimacy in that almost silence. I think it is then, in that moment, that all poetry begins, in a moment like the one described in this David Lehman poem from his book *Valentine Place:*

Dutch Interior

He liked the late afternoon light as it dimmed
In the living room, and wouldn't switch on
The electric lights until past eight o'clock.
His wife complained, called him cheerless, but
It wasn't a case of melancholy; he just liked
The way things looked in the air growing darker
So gradually and imperceptibly that it seemed
The very element in which we live. Every man
And woman deserves one true moment of greatness
And this was his, this Dutch interior, entered
And possessed, so tranquil and yet so busy
With details: the couple's shed clothes scattered
On the backs of armchairs, the dog chasing a shoe,
The wide open window, the late afternoon light.

ANTLER

Walt Whitman, *Leaves of Grass*
Jack London, *Martin Eden*
Henry David Thoreau, *Walden*
Robinson Jeffers, *Complete Poems*
Allen Ginsberg, *Complete Poems*
Charles Algernon Swinburne, *Complete Poems*
Percy Shelley, *Complete Poems*
Olaf Stapledon, *The Star Maker*
François Rabelais, *Gargantua and Pantagruel*
William Shakespeare, *Hamlet*

Walt Whitman became my best friend when I was a boy and had no close friend and was yearning desperately for one, and *Leaves of Grass* unfolded a vision of love and death and nature that seemed more beautiful and true to me than the Bible or any sacred text from any spiritual tradition.

Martin Eden was *the* book that inspired me to become a writer and to risk all to fulfill that call.

Walden first turned me on to the idea of the vision quest alone in Wilderness as a rite of passage (beyond human gurus and teachers) necessary for my poet-soul realization.

Jeffers' towering work affirmed and confirmed the deep, ecological, non-humancentric worldview that imbued my spirit early and ever since.

Ginsberg's vast contribution emboldened and emblazoned me for the challenge of grappling in poetry with the injustice, intolerance, and inhumanity of our society—with uncompromising intensity but tinged with hope and compassion and also celebrating, as Whitman did, the promise of same-sex love.

Swinburne's poems confronting Christianity and replacing it with Greek mythology, goddess worship, and nature mysticism were the first I read that did so and riveted me with determination to be unafraid to speak my heart.

Shelley empowered and aroused me in the same way with his defiant boyish romantic ethereal individualism.

The Star Maker is the most incredible and expansive astronomical meditation I have ever read and has influenced the starry nightsky love in my work more than any other book.

Rabelais proved for me that triumph of humor and extended imaginative playful delight in exploring any subject, especially sexuality, at any length and on every level.

Hamlet was the great archetype for my melancholy teenage mind-space – the doomed young hero with noble soliloquy holding a skull up and contemplating it – which I have been doing ever since...

RAE ARMANTROUT

Emily Dickinson, *The Complete Poems*
William Carlos Williams, *Spring and All*
Robert Creeley, *Words*
Lorine Niedecker, *Complete Works*
John Ashbery, *Three Poems*
Francis Ponge, *The Voice of Things*
George Oppen, *Of Being Numerous*
Fanny Howe, *Selected Poems*
Ron Silliman, *Ketjak*
Lyn Hejinian, *My Life*

Whoever coined the term "dark energy" might have been thinking of Emily Dickinson. She "dances like a Bomb, abroad / and swings upon the Hours."

Spring and All combines poetry of minimalist precision with open-ended prose passages in which Williams mulls over issues in politics and poetics. There is nothing like it.

It's hard to choose one Creeley book–but *Words* shows Creeley at his edgy, take-no-prisoners best.

Niedecker's *Complete Works*, edited by Jenny Penberthy, is new–but I've been reading Niedecker for many years. The sonic texture of her poetry is extremely beautiful. Her poems, spare as they are, give a complex picture of human beings' relation to nature and to one another.

Three Poems was a revelation when it first came out. Ashbery was writing a new sort of prose poem which, in turn, demanded a new sort of reader–one with expanded negative capability.

Ponge's prose poems about objects ("The Potato," "The Orange") are absolutely unique. His depictions are both scientifically precise and comically allusive.

Oppen writes with great, stark dignity in *Of Being Numerous* about the course of American "civilization." I'm struck by the way his line often appears to stop short as if at the edge of some crevasse he thereby makes perceptible.

I've read all of Fanny Howe's books–and I'd recommend you do the same. If I have to choose, though, I'll hedge by choosing the *Selected*. Howe is a modern day Metaphysical poet–and she has the best ear since Lorine Niedecker.

Silliman's *Ketjak* broke open the idea of form in poetry. Form was no longer received and conventional. New forms could come forth.

Evolution was real!

In *My Life* Hejinian combines formal inventiveness with a brilliant exploration of epistemology and the psychology of perception. This is true of all her books–but *My Life* is a good place to start.

ANGELA BALL

Charles Simic, *Dismantling the Silence*
James Wright, *The Branch Will Not Break*
Elizabeth Bishop, *Geography III*
Jean Rhys, *Good Morning Midnight*
Anna Akhmatova, *Requiem*, trans. Judith Hemschemeyer

How does a book become—and remain—essential? By virtue, I believe, of the richness of its worldview, a response to experience that makes nothing impossible. We may start by loving the work, but end by loving the author: the Simic-ness of Simic, the Wright-ness of Wright, the Bishop-ness of Bishop, the Rhys-ness of Rhys, the Akhmatova-ness of Akhmatova. Authors transform themselves from names to constant presences, wholenesses.

It's no accident that the titles of Charles Simic's first collections (small press editions, the precursors of *Dismantling the Silence*) of poetry, *What the Grass Says* and *Somewhere Among Us a Stone Is Taking Notes*, both suggest a preternatural attentiveness. This world holds another one inside it: "Go inside a stone," Simic says, "That would be my way." His imagination renders the mythic and the down-to-earth one and the same. On first reading Simic's work in 1972, I was a star-struck. The next year, he visited Ohio University and I heard him read and talked to him afterward for a long time (which seemed—still seems—incredible good luck). From his poems I've learned that there's no such thing as being alone, because even the inanimate has its history.

Going to college, I lived at home with my parents and an older sister. We were a shy family. I became convinced that I would never know the life I imagined others were living: excitements, pleasures, dramas involving other people. What a mystery! And no way into it. One night, awake in my room, I read James Wright's *The Branch Will Not Break*. Growing up in Southeastern Ohio, I had shared a landscape with Wright—the sad, scarred, lovely hills. I had seen the river, the smoke stacks and furnaces beside it—satanic energies that built the little towns and ruined them, too. In "Stages on a Journey Westward" Wright remembers,

> I began in Ohio.
> I still dream of home.
> Near Mansfield, enormous dobbins enter dark barns in autumn,
> Where they can be lazy, where they can munch little apples,
> Or sleep long.

But by night now, in the bread lines my father
Prowls, I cannot find him: So far off,
1500 miles or so away, and yet
I can hardly sleep.
In a blue rag the old man limps to my bed,
Leading a blind horse,
Of gentleness.
In 1932, grimy with machinery, he sang me
A lullaby of a goosegirl.
Outside the house, the slag heaps waited.

Here was someone who understood loneliness, who had lived despair. His response to it–his faith in nature and in words–came home to me all at once in the second of "Two Hangovers":

Number Two:
I Try to Waken and Greet the World Once Again

In a pine tree,
A few yards away from my windowsill,
A brilliant blue jay is springing up and down, up and down,
On a branch.
I laugh, as I see him abandon himself
To entire delight, for he knows as well as I do
That the branch will not break.

A life of being alive to nature, of recording it in words, in poetry that knows what a bird knows, could be possible for me because of Wright's example. More and more now, I think of Wright as a poet who praises his vocation and delights in passing it along. The beautiful "Prayer to the Good Poet" (from *Two Citizens*) links Horace, Wright himself, and Wright's young son as part of the same long and generous conversation. Reading him, I knew that the loneliness which had seemed so final could be redeemed in words.

Elizabeth Bishop's final book, the great *Geography III*, testifies to the power of language over loss. We're all misplaced, displaced–our poor, struggling sense of self dependent on context, constantly disrupted by change. Bishop shows us that the kind of noticing done through language may not restore the things themselves, but does restore the memory of them. Memory makes art necessary, and art makes memory real. As Bishop's "One Art" tells us, poetry is "the art of losing." It's all one. For poetry, to record loss is to defeat it, to change it to celebration:

an assertion of what matters, what abides.

There's something else about Bishop–something I can't fully elaborate. The close observation of known facts leads always to mystery, a mystery that is as nourishing in its own strange way as the details we can cradle in our hands. It's in "a dim / smell of moose, an acrid / smell of gasoline" at the close of Bishop's "The Moose." It's what we spy when, tying our shoes, we "look into the earth" in Charles Simic's "Poem." It's the chill at the close of Wright's "Prayer to the Good Poet." The more I think about it, the more I know: books for me (and not just poetry, of course– novels and stories and plays) have been a way to loosen my construction of experience, to let me respond with something other than plain, bred-in-the-bone bewilderment and despair.

This brings me to Jean Rhys and her novel, *Good Morning Midnight*. Rhys found her vocation through a back door. After being discarded by her wealthy lover, Rhys the actress/chorus-girl/masseuse bought a notebook and colored pens and sat down to record her story, becoming a writer in the process. My poem-bio of her in my book *Quartet* imagines her saying:

> Only the books matter.
> If I stop writing my life
> It will have been a failure.
> I will not have earned death.
> Only writing is important, only books
> take you out of yourself.

Writing isn't only a way to escape the self, it's a way of exposing socially accepted hypocrisy. To do her experience justice, she enlisted the objectivity of craft. Far from a complaint or lament, Rhys' work is an indictment and a vindication. As my colleague Steven Barthelme says, "Next to Jean Rhys, everyone else is just kidding." In her introduction to *Jean Rhys: The Complete Novels*, Diana Athill declares:

> ...the writer must be able to stand back from the experience far enough to see the whole of it and must concentrate with a selfpurging intensity on the process of reproducing it in words. Jean Rhys could stand back, and her concentration on the process was as intense as that of a tightrope walker. As a result her novels do not say 'This is what happened to me,' but 'This is how things happen.'

In *Good Morning Midnight,* the book I think of as quintessential

Rhys, we hear the world through the voice of Sasha, a woman who has been abandoned. We see what it's like to live beyond the pale and beneath contempt, a world where women have two universally recognized identities: wife or prostitute. Rhys' stories and novels have the gall, the ever-lasting nerve, to see and record things as themselves rather than frosting them with some sort of doily.

Anna Akhmatova, the last of my essential authors, is the ultimate truth teller. She lived under the tyrant Stalin, in a time when truth too often meant death. In Judith Hemschemeyer's translation, *Requiem* begins:

> In the terrible years of the Yezhov terror, I spent seventeen months in the prison lines of Leningrad. Once, someone 'recognized' me. Then a woman with bluish lips standing behind me, who, of course, had never heard me called by name before, woke up from the stupor to which everyone had succumbed and whispered in my ear (everyone spoke in whispers there):
>
> 'Can you describe this?'
>
> And I answered: 'Yes, I can.'
>
> Then something that looked like a smile passed over what had once been her face.

From Akhmatova, true saint of poetry, I learned that memory is a moral imperative: the last and best defense against evil. That whatever else happens, we have language, with truth's power embedded in it like a tornado in a thunderstorm.

So this is my testament, my recommendation. If you haven't had the happiness of these writers yet, I wish it for you. It's our fine luck that they exist and have given us these books to remember ourselves by.

MARVIN BELL

Allen Ginsberg, *Howl*
Robert Creeley, *For Love*
William Carlos Williams, *Spring and All*
William Carlos Williams, *Collected Poems* (2 vols)
William Stafford, *Traveling Through the Dark*
Ezra Pound, *ABC of Reading*
Wallace Stevens, *Harmonium*
John Logan, *Spring of the Thief*
Donald Justice, *Selected Poems*
Selected Poems of Pablo Neruda and César Vallejo, trans. Robert Bly

My list is random, arbitrary, seat-of-the-pants, and altogether ad-lib. It's 10 p.m. Pacific Savings Time on July 30, 2003, in Port Townsend, Washington, and I have spent only two minutes on this because it can only be a sampler. No way can I choose only 5-10 books and say they were: "most influential." I could make a different list for each year, sometimes for each month. These books knocked my socks off, but so did a hundred others.

Okay, so I put *Howl* on the list because I used to cut graduate journalism classes to go with two friends to an Italian restaurant in Syracuse where we read the Beats. I was never going to be a proper academic, and who swept the academic aside better than Ginsberg? He also stood in for Whitman. And Creeley, who also stood in for Emily Dickinson, for his sense of interval. And WCW's *Spring & All* because it is the single book I took to Spain. Also, Williams' poems as now collected in a two-volume set because Dr. Williams was the busiest of poets and a helpless genius of words (as Stevens was a calculating genius) and could say, and had to say: "Only one solution: to write carelessly so that nothing that is not green will survive." And William Stafford's first nationally-distributed book because its voice is, as the National Book Award judges said, "tough and gentle," and Bill understood and displayed as well as anyone the freedom available to a poet. Pound's *ABC* because he had the long view and thus could repeat things such as this, quoting from, he says, Coleridge or De Quincey (he is himself not sure which): "The quality of a great poet is everywhere present but nowhere visible as a distinct excitement." Stevens' first book because it is a baroque achievement that proves Wittgenstein's assertion that one can avoid saying a false thing only by means of nonsense or tautology. And John Logan's most beautiful book because he had the best reading voice of his generation and wrote for it. And Donald Justice because his poetry proves that precision is moving. Finally, a sampler of Neruda and Vallejo, translated and mistranslated by Bly, to stand in for a hundred poets from other countries, because world poetry is bigger than just American poetry or poetry in English, and one must take heart and permission from other cultures.

CHARLES BERNSTEIN

FOUR SEASONS

I.
1. Heraclitus, [fragments]
2. Plato, *Cratylus*
3. Lucretius, *De Rerum Natura*
4. Augustine, *Confessions*
5. Descartes, *Meditations*
6. Spinoza, *Ethics*
7. Leibniz, *Monadology*
8. Rousseau, *Emile*
9. Wollstonecraft, *A Vindication of the Rights of Women*
10. Kierkegaard, *Philosophical Fragments*
11. Nietzche, *The Genealogy of Morals*
12. Marx, "The Eighteenth Brumaire of Louis Napoleon"
13. Wilde, *The Decay of Lying*

II.
1. Adorno, *Negative Dialectics*
2. Habermas, *Knowledge and Human Interest*
3. Hillberg, *The Destruction of the European Jews*
4. Foucault, *Power/Knowledge*
5. Althusser, "Ideology and Ideological State Apparatuses"
6. Erving Goffman, *Frame Analysis*
7. Irigaray, *This Sex Which Is Not One*
8. Benjamin, "Doctrine of the Similar"
9. Cavell, *The Senses of Walden*
10. Barthes, *Writing Degree Zero*
11. Wittgenstein, *Philosophical Investigations*
12. Freud, *The Psychopathology of Everyday Life*
13. Weil, *Gravity and Grace*

III.
1. Poe
2. Dickinson
3. Hawthorne
4. Whitman
5. Melville
6. Emerson

7. Thoreau
8. H. James
9. Stein
10. Eliot
11. Pound
12. Williams
13. Stevens

IV.
1. *The New American Poetry: 1945-1960*, ed. Donald Allen

2. *From the Other Side of the Century: A New American Poetry, 1960-1990*, ed. Douglas Messerli; &, also edited by Messleri, *Language Poetries: An Anthology*

3. *Revolution of the Word: A New Gathering of American Avant Garde Poetry 1914-1945*, ed. Jerome Rothenberg; &, also edited by Rothenberg, *Technicians of the Sacred: A Range of Poetries from Africa, America, Asia, Europe and Oceania*

4. *American Poetry: The Twentieth Century*, vols. 1 and 2 (New York: The Library of America, 2000)

5. *In the American Tree: Language, Realism, Poetry*, ed. Ron Silliman

6. *SHI: A Radical Reading of Chinese Poetry*, Yunte Huang

7. *Postmodern American Poetry: A Norton Anthology*, ed. Paul Hoover

8. *Poems for the Millennium: The University of California Books of Modern and Postmodern Poetry*, vols. 1 and 2, ed. Jerome Rothenberg and Pierre Joris

9. *500 Years of Latin American Poetry: A Bilingual Anthology*, ed. Cecilia Vicuna and Ernesto Grosman

10. *The Random House Book of Twentieth Century French Poetry*, ed. Paul Auster; *The Yale Anthology of Twentieth-Century French Poetry*, ed. Mary Ann Caws

11. *Moving Borders: Three Decades of Innovative Writing by Women*, ed. Mary Margaret Sloan

12. *Out of Everywhere: An Anthology of Contemporary Linguistically Innovative Poetry by Women in North America & the UK*, ed. Maggie O'Sullivan

13. *Anthology of Twentieth-Century British and Irish Poetry*, ed. Keith Tuma; *Other: British and Irish Poetry since 1970*, ed. Richard Caddel and Peter Quartermain

SUPPLEMENT

Two collections I edited: *43 Poets (1984) (boundary* 2, 1987*)* and *99 Poets/1999: An International Poetics Symposium (boundary* 2, 1999, available as a book from Duke University Press); & two key web sites: ubu.com & epc.buffalo.edu.

ANSELM BERRIGAN

Kevin Davies, *Comp.*
Harryette Mullen, *Muse & Drudge*
Douglas Oliver, *A Salvo for Africa*
John Ashbery, *Wakefulness*
Amiri Baraka, *Transbluesency*
Emily Dickinson, *Final Harvest*
Philip Whalen, *Overtime: Selected Poems*
Alice Notley, *Mysteries of Small Houses*
Alice Notley, *Disobedience*
Samuel Taylor Coleridge, *The Complete Poems*
Eileen Myles, *Not Me*

In putting together this list I chose the books that I feel have most strongly impacted my writing in the last five years or so. I could easily include the poetry of my father (Ted Berrigan) and brother (Edmund Berrigan), but for the sake of avoiding a list dominated by my family I've decided to just mention them here. What links these books in my imagination is the simple fact that each book makes me want to write (makes writing poetry feel possible), and each poet has taught me something important about writing on technical and emotional levels.

I chose *Final Harvest* by Emily Dickinson not because it is the most comprehensive collection of her work, but because I have this beat up copy that I found in the early nineties in an old bookstore in Buffalo, New York and have held onto ever since. Dickinson was the first poet I read whose work I identified with instinctively (aside from family). I loved the fact that she used these dashes and irregular capitalization to disrupt any kind of pat formalism that might have taken over her work, and I felt an immediate sense of closeness to the writing when I came across lines like "I felt a funeral in my brain." In an odd way, I associate her with the rock band Sonic Youth, whose use of feedback and distortion in much of their work both complements and takes apart the structure of pop songs.

Kevin Davies' *Comp.* is a funny, angry book with an impeccable sense of timing. It is difficult to describe what Davies is doing in brief, but one of his strengths is his ability to take political and emotional content and render it humorously and effectively without resorting to polemics and without relying on standard narrative techniques. Davies is also especially adept at taking dense subject matter and treating it with great linguistic flexibility as well as literal clarity. The work in *Comp.* has a satirical bent (with a focus on slogans), but is also operating well outside the confines of that genre.

Muse & Drudge is a book-length poem which aided me immensely in my own efforts to write longer poems. In an interview in *Combo* magazine, Mullen talked about *Muse & Drudge* as a conscious attempt on her part to create a work that could bring both of her audiences as she perceived them at the time–the mostly black audience that was interested in her early, more narrative work and the mostly white audience that took to her experimental writing–into the same room. Mullen's music in *Muse & Drudge*, drawn from a wide range of sources including blues, rap, and playground songs and chatter, is at once a deep and successful experiment with polyvocality and a relentless (and, often, joyous) sweep of rhythm and form (the poem is in irregularly rhymed quatrains).

A Salvo for Africa, written by the British poet Douglas Oliver (my stepfather), is important to me for personal reasons, obviously, but is also a kind of book that I don't believe I've ever seen anywhere else. Doug meticulously researched the history, politics, and culture of dozens of African nations in order to write poems to a Western audience, specifically Britain, to address what he called "the failure of imagination" endemic to the West in its view of Africa. Doug shed his more innovative styles of writing (for him poetic styles and forms were meant to be studied, inhabited, and moved on from in order to keep one fresh and motivated) in order to, as he put it, "risk prose." Thus each poem in the book is complemented by a passage of prose relevant to the country about which the poem is written. It is a book that is difficult for many people to deal with, for a wide variety of reasons; it is also an incredibly smart, compassionate, and uncynical book which knows exactly whom it is talking to and why, and that in itself is an incredible rarity among poetry books.

John Ashbery's *Wakefulness* and Amiri Baraka's *Transbluesency* (a kind of large selected poems) are linked, in a way, in my imagination. Both of these guys have published millions of books and are obviously poetic geniuses, but what I get from them in the above books is a sense of the art of arrangement within a poem; the artful arrangement of thought, to be more precise. *Wakefulness* appeals to me more than Ashbery's other recent books because, I think, the combination of mystery, humor, and impeccable phrasing just came together in my imagination in total sync. I've nearly destroyed my copy of that book from carrying it around too much. In Baraka's case, I've been particularly interested in his ability to use sharp, sometimes frightening language and still leave it clear that one is *looking* at such language being used as well as reading it–many of Baraka's poems from the late fifties and sixties strike me as objects testing the reader's ability to receive information as art. And if there is overwhelming rage and/or pain, say, on the surface of a poem like "Black Dada Nihilismus," there is also an incredibly measured and acute intellect at work that demands more than an emotional reaction to that surface.

Overtime: Selected Poems of Philip Whalen is likely the easiest book of Whalen's to find, and certainly an excellent selected poems. All of his books are worth reading, since there is a lot of work left out of *Overtime* (which is nonetheless a three hundred page volume). From Whalen I have learned a great deal about spacing on the page and how using the whole of the page (putting words anywhere rather than always retreating to the left margin) can allow a writer to really track one's consciousness ("a graph of the mind moving," as Whalen put it once). That said, Whalen's work is not automatic writing–it is carefully nuanced and deeply informed by Zen Buddhism in ways that I am not qualified to even begin to explain. One thing about Whalen's work that has always interested me is the fact that his own work can be read quickly, but he always seems to be taking his time within the poems. His pacing is a combination of deliberate and quick thought and observation (there's a feeling that one is taking a walk with him in his poems, particularly the longer pieces).

The two books I've listed by Alice Notley (my mother), *Mysteries of Small Houses* and *Disobedience*, were published back-to-back in 1999 and 2001, respectively. *Mysteries of Small Houses* is an autobiography in poems, though it wasn't intended to be such when she started it. Her idea was to "recenter" the I in her poems, and to take on self-investigation and self-recognition without any trappings, for lack of a better way to put it. The book reads as autobiography, but each poem takes on a different style and the stylistic changes tend to mark the passage of time by reflecting the sensibility of each period she's writing from (i.e. Iowa in the early seventies, a childhood in the Mojave Desert, New York City in the eighties, etc.). Thus the poems span her life but are not frozen in reflection; rather, they are emotionally and tonally rich and fierce at once, and absolutely present in mind. *Disobedience* is a long poem (made of shorter pieces) and a definite departure from *Mysteries*. *Disobedience* combines elements of the detective novel (as embodied by a character modeled after Robert Mitchum), a heavy use of dream imagery, and the politics of globalization as seen through the eyes of a fifty-year-old American woman who has expatriated herself from the U.S. to live in France. Because the material is very close to me personally it is harder to say what I've learned from these books. The fact of the matter is, when I read someone's books more than several times I think I begin to absorb more information than I can immediately recognize. For instance, it took me several years to realize that I had learned a great deal about poetry–how to begin and end a line, say–by reading my parents' books before I started writing seriously. I was looking for biographical information, but I was also unconsciously taking in the way their poems were shaped, and their senses of timing, rhythm and humor. That said, dynamic control of one's "I" without resorting to rote confessionalism or prosaic posturing is perhaps the strongest thing I've gained from Notley's books.

Coleridge's work has meant a lot to me for a few different reasons. One being that through his poetry and its unabashed exploration of the imagination I was able to find a way into really looking closely at British poetry of the nineteenth century and earlier. Coleridge has a remarkably generous and gregarious spirit, and it is not surprising to me now that I would find a way into other poets' work through his sensibility at a time when I was suspicious, to say the least, of much of what is considered canonical work. I've also found Coleridge's poems such as "This Lime Tree Bower My Prison" to be slightly distant precursors to the work of 20th century poets I love, Frank O'Hara in particular. While each poet's work is quite different, especially in terms of diction, both poets take on friendship as extensive subject matter and as a source of inspiration and exuberance. Coleridge is also a poet whose work I've used to try and understand my own experiences with several of the emotional and psychological states he wrote through, including dejection, grief, wonder, compassion, and addiction. As with Dickinson, the Penguin edition I've mentioned is the one I have, and not the only or best edition available, necessarily. The Romantic biographer Richard Holmes has written a truly brilliant and readable two-volume biography of Coleridge that covers both his work and life, and I strongly recommend both volumes.

Finally, Eileen Myles' *Not Me*, another book which I have in a completely dog-eared, beat up edition, is a book in which Myles boldly remade the New York School aesthetic of walking around the city and soaking it all in with wit and nerve into her own vehicle, one that she drives with stark authority and toughness. Myles' New York in *Not Me* is the dangerous and dirty (though nonetheless beautiful) New York of the seventies and eighties. Myles makes extensive use of a short line and a kind of James Schuyler-esque long column, and it was initially that form and its inherent quickness that I was attracted to, along with Myles' guts. "An American Poem," in which she "comes out" as a member of the Kennedy family, is a totally hilariously willful poem that Myles used to help launch a presidential campaign in 1992. *Not Me* has a very distinct talking voice, and its insistence has been an influence on my own sense of tone as well as an example of how to maintain a kind of speech in poetry that sounds like a person talking while not reigned in by its own effect.

EAVAN BOLAND

Tillie Olsen, *Silences*
Charlotte Mew, *Collected Poems*
William Butler Yeats, *Collected Poems*
Adrienne Rich, *The Fact of a Doorframe*
Marcel Proust, *Remembrance of Things Past*
Vera Brittain, *Testament of Youth*
James Joyce, *Dubliners*
Alfred, Lord Tennyson, *In Memoriam*
Lord Byron, *Childe Harolde*
Sylvia Plath, *Ariel*

Most of these books have been companions to me for years. All of them have a special meaning, a special chronology in my life.

Tillie Olsen's *Silences* was the first eloquent cartography of exclusions I read as a younger woman.

Adrienne Rich's *The Fact of a Doorframe* gave me a solid view of her strength and achievement.

James Joyce's *Dubliners*, which I first found as a teenager–though it would have been difficult as a young Dubliner not to find it–transformed my own city for me into a new and exotic breviary of estrangement.

Vera Brittain's *Testament of Youth* is an account of the First World War written by a young woman who lost her fiancé and brother at the Front. Its powerful journal-like writing made me see for the first time a concept which has become increasingly important to me: the power of the public event glimpsed through an entirely private lens.

Both Tennyson and Byron are poets I keep with me–both out of place in their centuries: Byron a migrant from the eighteenth century, Tennyson a melancholy harbinger of the twentieth. Their lyrical, off-kilter poems are ones I always return to.

Remembrance of Things Past shows Marcel Proust's beautiful, alternative world–apparently located in a time and place, but really a piece of timeless elegy. This may be my favorite of all books.

Yeats is here because the power of his work, its light and courage, were the first pieces of information I really took in about the dignity of being an Irish poet.

Charlotte Mew's *Collected Poems* for its evocation of a dark England: her poems have a rare and unswerving music of abandonment and lyric dissidence.

And finally, Plath's *Ariel* is here because there always has to be one book to remind us how much we have lost.

CATHERINE BOWMAN

Ovid, *The Metamorphoses of Ovid*
Gwendolyn Brooks, *Selected Poems*
Charles Simic, *Return to a Place Lit by a Glass of Milk*
C. D. Wright, *Steal Away: Selected and New Poems*
The Poetry of Pablo Neruda
C. P. Cavafy, *Collected Poems,* trans. Edmund Keeley
The Holy Bible
*No More Masks: An Anthology of 20ᵗʰ Century American Women
        Writers*, ed. Florence Howe
Joseph Brodsky, *Less than One: Selected Essays*
Elizabeth Bishop, *The Complete Poems*

Recently, someone asked me why I write and not really knowing how to answer I said, "To get me into trouble and get me out of trouble." Maybe that is why I read as well. The list of books above, among many others, have been essential reading for me, getting me into trouble and out of trouble at different times in my life, for different reasons, acting in my imagination as ready accomplices and sturdy life boats.

ALAN CATLIN

Allen Ginsberg, *Howl and Other Poems*
Allen Ginsberg, *Kaddish*
T. S. Eliot, "The Waste Land"
Wilfred Owen, *The Collected Poems*
Michael Casey, *Obscenities*
Federico García Lorca, *Poet in New York*
Carolyn Forché, *The Country Between Us*
Sharon Olds, *The Dead and the Living*
Michael Ondaatje, *The Collected Works of Billy the Kid*
Cid Corman, *Sun Rock Man*
William Bronk, *Life Supports*

I think of *Howl* and *Kaddish* in conjunction, as inseparable from each other. The words literally leap off the page. Poetry from the point of their publication was forever changed. Ginsberg freed poetry from the bonds of artificial forms and conventions and allowed the poet to become part (subject) of the poetic process.

Despite Eliot's obvious faults as a human being, in "The Waste Land" he managed (with Pound's indispensable help–anyone who doubts his influence on Eliot need only look at the facsimile manuscript for confirmation) to write the signature poem of his generation. "The Waste Land" coupled with "The Hollow Men" and "The Love Song of J. Alfred Prufrock" bring us from a 19th century sensibility to the Modern Age.

In his war poems, like "Anthem for the Doomed Youth," Wilfred Owen describes senseless slaughter in the name of a just war in visceral, lyrical poems from the soldier's point of view in a way that had never been seen before. Need I say more?

In *Obscenities*, through his Everyman persona, Dufus, Michael Casey brings our senseless Vietnam experiment in the terror of war home in everyday language. If for nothing else, Casey should be celebrated for the closure of his poem, "A Bummer":

> If you have a farm in Vietnam
> And a house in hell
> Sell the farm
> And go home.

In *Poet in New York*, García Lorca brings his sensitive eye to an urban setting as a keen observer of our alien urban culture. Few, if any, observers so compactly and accurately captured the American ethos as García Lorca did in this groundbreaking duende for the modern urban dweller.

The Country Between Us is Forché's now classic observation of life under the rule of CIA sponsored dictatorships in Latin America noted for their brutality, prison encampments and human rights violations. It's told with an unflinching eye. Hearing and seeing Forché read "The Colonel," among others in this collection, is a transformative experience:

> The colonel returned with a sack used to bring
> groceries home. He spilled many human ears on the
> table. They were like dried peach halves. There is
> no other way to say this.

In *The Dead and the Living* Sharon Olds' work resonates with personal honesty and immediacy, making Art from personal pain. Her work is often brutal but always compassionate, showing that she is driven by work that transforms, that makes a person better for having confronted the most difficult personal issues rather than succumbing to them or indulging the pain for pain's sake. While Olds often works on the same kinds of subjects and passions as the seminal poet of her generation, Sylvia Plath, she moves beyond the demons of Plath's "Ariel" in order to help others, hence "The Dead and the Living."

Ondaatje's *The Collected Works of Billy the Kid* is a novel in poetic form, a vast collage of articles, pictures, observations, accounts and poems that show just how flexible the poetic form can be.

I chose *Sun Rock Man* from Cid Corman's work only because it was the first of his books I was exposed to and because it opened the proverbial door to his vast corpus of Zen inspired poetry. He has the uncommon gift of compression for effect that is unrivaled by any other modern poet.

The After Thought

> Like old women
> gabbling at the
> sidelot beside
>
> the restaurant
> with chickens trussed
> under their arms.

There's much to do
about doing
what isn't done.

William Bronk's *Life Supports*: This collection of selected poetry from the undervalued poet of his generation (along with Simon Perchik) brought some recognition to the premier philosophical poet of the second half of the 20th century. Bronk is another poet, like Corman, though he eschews the images of the latter, who had an incredible gift for compression for effect.

HENRI COLE

Frank Bidart, *Sacrifice*
Elizabeth Bishop, *Geography III*
Anne Carson, *Autobiography of Red*
Amy Clampitt, *What the Light Was Like*
Louise Glück, *Ararat*
Louise Glück, *The Triumph of Achilles*
Thom Gunn, *The Man with Nightsweats*
Seamus Heaney, *North*
James Merrill, *Nights and Days*
May Swenson, *The Complete Poems of May Swenson*
Derek Walcott, *The Star-Apple Kingdom*

I've chosen to recommend books by contemporary poets.

The two biggest influences on my work are sleeping and reading. I wish I could do them simultaneously. They make the little hamster of the unconscious run wild on its wheel.

I love Louise Glück; her work illuminates what all art must, those great human subjects, which she identifies as "time which breeds loss, desire, the world's beauty." I love May Swenson for her absence of narcissism and her childlike wonder before nature and sexuality. I love Elizabeth Bishop for her use of description as narrative, dramatizing feeling. And Seamus Heaney for remaining socially responsible and creatively free.

My list should also include books by John Koethe and Charles Wright. And how about Wislawa Szymborska! She is a giant wearing a little mortal mask.

WANDA COLEMAN

Robinson Jeffers, *Selected Poems*
César Vallejo, *Trilce,* trans. David Smith
Bob Kaufman, *Solitudes Crowded with Loneliness*
The Voice That is Great Within Us: American Poetry of The Twentieth
    Century, ed. Hayden Carruth
Charles Baudelaire, *Flowers of Evil*
You Better Believe it: Black Verse in English, ed. Paul Breman (favoring
    the poems by James Weldon Johnson, Claude McKay,
    A.B. Spellman and Bob Kaufman)
E. E. Cummings, *Complete Poems, 1913-1962*
Kenneth Fearing, *New and Selected Poems*
John Ashbery, *Self-Portrait in a Convex Mirror*
Charles Bukowski, *The Days Run Away like Wild Horses Over the Hills*

> Night comes: night will claim all.
> The world is not changed, only more naked:
> The strong struggle for power, and the weak
> Warm their poor hearts with hate.
> > –from "Watch the Lights Fade," Robinson Jeffers

Leaving out most of the anthologies, the fiction, philosophy, and sociology–and being too poor to afford books for most of my life, I do not own many of the books by poets who have influenced me (such as Edna St. Vincent Millay–a high school favorite, Olson's *The Maximus Poems*, Pound's *Cantos*, and Robert Duncan), or only recently acquired them (such as the collected works of Brother Antoninus or William Everson). They were either borrowed from public libraries or from the private collections of friends and mentors. Of the books I own, that I return to again and again to refresh myself, these are the most dog-eared in order of preference.

Jeffers' poetic sensibility is so foreign to my own, I'm uncertain as to why I love his work, except that I feel his soul moving beneath his text, a quality I admire. His voice is distinct, and I feel as though he's alive in his words–living. And I can feel his earthly movements about a fiercely beautiful terrain.

I can't help but empathize with the repressed strength that emerges from the pages of *Trilce* and pierces the translations.

Kaufman's skewed jazzy jive, conundrums, reverse logic, and risky surrealism sometimes move from fun to fury within the space of a line– counteracting his self-deprecation and often-forced moments. I've longed to do a 'graphic translation' of his work, because I don't think his line breaks are very well represented in much of his work, and some of his rhythms are misheard.

Baudelaire is aesthetic kindred.

I know I'm presumed to like African American poetry, but I find most of it written prior to the 1970s terribly uninteresting, and embarrassingly bad and corny (like most African American visual art), and imitative of better craftsmen of the Caucasian persuasion for the obvious reasons; however, some of the finest of what's excellent in diverse Black voices is found in *You Better Believe It*. Sorry, but I'm not a big fan of Langston Hughes, even if I respect his "contribution" and voted for the stamp. I was invited to contribute to this anthology back in the day, but my naiveté and paranoia (at the time) kept me from submitting work. I'm now glad that I didn't, because at that time my fledgling work was as bad as some of the worst in this collection. Thank goodness, I don't have to live that down. Whew.

From Cummings, i take my stylistic use of the lower case not from a sense of inferiority (because i've never felt inferior to ANYONE in my life, although plenty of snotty literary folk of all persuasions have tried to make me feel that way). i also like his use of parentheses, although i part company with him on the semicolon.

Kenneth Fearing: as a man trapped in his time, savoring his class, his observer's eye (as good as Nathaniel West's), his wry-to-tipsy romance-tinged spinnings are a delight to encounter and sound out loud.

Ashbery's *Self-Portrait in a Convex Mirror* is just a bloody good 'n' smart little book, choice lines, makes me keep saying "of course." Who'd ever think of saying: "The dark is waiting like so many other things, dumbness and voluptuousness among them"?

When the pretentious dreck and sappy pseudo-philosophy that seem to impress most Americans as poetry get to be too much, I go running and screaming for a dose of Charles "Hank" Bukowski—although he is not without pretensions of his own, his are just more forgivable. It is because of his flawed, and therefore thoroughly human, point-of-view (and Barbara Martin's covers) that I was drawn to Black Sparrow Press, and dared submit my fledgling manuscript. Too, he was the only living poet of note on the L. A. scene that I was able to access and observe, other than Henri Coulette and John Thomas. (I did catch Deena Metzger at the Haymarket and Stuart Perkoff at Venice West.) Tom McGrath had already been run out of town. I was at Hank's first poetry reading, and was the only thing black or female in the room. I still have the flyer.

There are so many more—Cavafy, Lorca, Neruda, and Plath among the more notable. But, perhaps another time, another survey.

CLARK COOLIDGE

Jack Kerouac, *Old Angel Midnight*, the first 49 sections as printed in
  Big Table magazine, no. 1, 1959.

Jack Spicer, *The Heads of the Town Up to the Aether* (1962)

Larry Eigner, *On My Eyes* (1960)

William Carlos Williams, *Spring and All*, just the poems, as printed in
  the *Collected Earlier Poems*, from New Directions, available in
  the late Fifties. I didn't see the complete text, with prose, until
  the Frontier Press edition of 1970.

Philip Whalen, *Memoirs of an Interglacial Age* (1960)

John Ashbery, *The Tennis Court Oath* (1962) I had previously seen the
  poem "Europe" in *Big Table* 4, 1960.

Joe Ceravolo, *Fits of Dawn* (1965)

Gregory Corso, *Gasoline* (1958)

Philip Lamantia, *Destroyed Works* (1962)

Ted Berrigan, *The Sonnets* (1964)

Charles Olson, *The Distances* (1960)

Louis Zukofsky, *Some Time* (1956) I didn't actually own this book until LZ
  gave me a copy in the early Sixties. I had previously seen the "Songs
  of Degrees" in one of the last issues of the *Black Mountain Review*.

Robert Creeley, *For Love* (1962)

Bill Berkson, *Saturday Night* (1961)

Ray Bremser, *Drive Suite* (1968) The poem was written in 1960. I was
  given a copy of Ray's typescript by Buell Neidlinger, Cecil
  Taylor's bass player in the fifties, in 1961.

Michael McClure, *Hymns to St. Geryon* (1959)

The publication dates are, unless otherwise indicated, also the
years of first possession.

I do not intend this list as any sort of "canon." This is the
contemporary American poetry that most excited me as I began to seriously
attempt the art.

JIM DANIELS

Lawrence Ferlinghetti, *A Coney Island of the Mind*
Tom Kromer, *Waiting for Nothing*
Jim Harrison, *Letters to Yesenin*
A Government Job at Last, ed. Tom Wayman
Louis Ferdinand Céline, *Journey to the Center of the Night*
Galway Kinnell, *Book of Nightmares*
Adam Hammer, *Deja Everything*
Guillevic, *Euclidians*, trans. Teo Savory
Nicanor Parra, *Emergency Poems*

A Coney Island of the Mind was the first book I read by a living poet, when I was a senior in high school. It turned my head around—at the time, I had a teacher telling me that what I was writing was poetry. But I did not like poetry—or, I didn't like the way poetry had been taught to me up until that point. It did not seem to connect to my life. It seemed intimidating and foreign. Ferlinghetti's beat, hipster voice was just what I needed to hear. It was incredibly exciting to know I could sound like myself, write in my voice, and sound musical in a jazzy way, as opposed to the stiff, formal rhythms of a lot of the classic poetry we were reading in school.

In a poem like "Christ Climbed Down," Ferlinghetti has this irreverence toward organized religion that I was incredibly hungry for at the time. Two of my first creative pieces were titled, "The Existence of God," and "The Existence of God, Part 2." Ferlinghetti showed how to write about God and religion without lapsing into abstract, philosophical ramblings:

> Christ climbed down
> from His bare Tree
> this year
> and ran away to where
> there were no rootless Christmas trees
> hung with candycanes and breakable stars

Waiting for Nothing was originally published in 1935. The first copy I read was a ragged xeroxed copy, for the book had been out of print for many years. Kromer's autobiographical novel of homelessness during the Great Depression taught me about the power of simple language and the value of repetition and rhythm. The opening paragraph of the novel captures the power of this unusual voice:

It is night. I am walking along this dark street, when my foot hits a stick. I reach down and pick it up. I finger it. It is a good stick, a heavy stick. One sock from it would lay a man out. It wouldn't kill him, but it would lay him out. I plan. Hit him where the crease is in his hat, hard, I tell myself, but not too hard. I do not want his head to hit the concrete. It might kill him. I do not want to kill him. I will catch him as he falls. I can frisk him in a minute. I will pull him over in the shadows and walk off. I will not run. I will walk.

It is nearly the cadences of the old Dick and Jane readers, yet in this grim, gripping story, it functions to punctuate the basic day-to-day survival of its narrator. As a poet, I was very interested in seeing, through voice, how much he could convey using very simple language, in seeing how much a writing style could influence the tone and mood of a piece, in seeing how repetition could convey an obsessive, unrelenting, and finally claustrophobic atmosphere.

As an undergraduate in college, while dealing with the break up of my first serious romance, I read Harrison's *Letters to Yesenin*. I was half-heartedly suicidal when I read Harrison's letter poems to Sergei Yesenin, the Russian poet who wrote his last poem in his own blood before killing himself. The complex textual layers of these prose poems was a revelation to me:

We're nearing the end of this homage that often resembles a suicide note to a suicide. I didn't mean it that way but how often our hands sneak up on our throats and catch us unaware. What are you doing here we say. Don't squeeze so hard.

Harrison revealed to me how to write unsentimentally about sentimental subjects. I mean, what on the surface could seem more maudlin than a suicide note to a suicide? I was humorlessly wallowing in the self-pity of someone who has not truly suffered when I read this book. The dignity and humor of these self-deprecating, heartbreaking poems showed me that I had a lot to learn–both about life, and poetry.

While *A Government Job at Last* is an anthology, it's an anthology with a clear vision: that in our poetry, work deserves to be treated as seriously as any other subject. Tom Wayman, a distinguished and prolific poet from Canada, has since edited other anthologies of poems about work, and written many fine essays on the subject as well. I was in graduate school at Bowling Green State University when I came across this book. At the time, I was writing many poems about working in a Ford axle plant near Detroit and bringing them into the workshop, where they met with a mixed response. It was heartening to read the wide range of voices in Wayman's selections, and to feel I had a home there, that it was okay to write poems about work, particularly blue-collar work.

In addition, the straightforward narrative structure of many of the poems in that anthology matched my style at the time, and gave me confidence that my poems could survive without a great deal of figurative language. The immediacy of the work experiences seemed to require more than the lyric, contemplative style that seemed to dominate the poetry world back then.

Journey to the Center of the Night: another novel. I published *Places/Everyone*, my first book of poems, in 1985, and someone said I should read Céline. This is what I read:

> The greatest defeat, in anything, is to forget, and above all to forget what it is that has smashed you, and to let yourself be smashed without ever realizing how thoroughly devilish men can be. When our time is up, we mustn't bear malice, but neither must we forget: we must tell the whole thing, without altering one word,–everything that we have seen of man's viciousness; and then it will be over and time to go. That is enough of a job for a whole lifetime.

Many of the poems in that first book were work poems set in Detroit's factories. I was already teaching at Carnegie Mellon University when the book came out, and some reviews of *Places/Everyone* suggested that now that I was teaching in a university, I would move beyond the factory to other subjects. Also, when I was interviewed on "All Things Considered," the reporter asked what beauty I found in the factory, as if poetry could only be about beauty. Céline's book, and this quote in particular, inspired me to continue writing about the world I grew up in, to not feel that I *had* to move on to other subjects, or start looking for beauty. It also reminded me of the political side of things, and it was a spur not to make my work seem more palatable to what one might imagine was a more general audience. Céline's wicked sense of humor, while puncturing the artifice and greed of our culture, was also inspiring.

Kinnell's *Book of Nightmares* taught me about poetic ambition. I have written three long poems, but I don't think I could have ever written one without reading *Book of Nightmares*. While I obviously have not written anything approaching *Book of Nightmares*, the long poems I have written were certainly inspired by Kinnell's example. In 1977, as an undergraduate,

I attended the Cranbrook Writers Conference in Michigan, at which Galway Kinnell was the guest poet. After his reading on the final day of the conference, I went to buy a book and have him sign it, but all the books were sold out. I went up to him and told him what a great reading it had been, and mentioned the books being sold out. Later at the reception, he walked up to me and handed me the copy of *Book of Nightmares* he'd read from, inscribed to me.

While that gesture taught me loads about grace and class, the book itself is as important as the gesture. *Book of Nightmares* is a book I have returned to again and again, and each reading yields more surprises and discoveries. What impresses me about the book is the combination of clarity and depth. It's both an incredibly sensual and an incredibly intellectual book. I learned that it takes big poems sometimes to handle big subjects. It doesn't seem long, and that's a key to writing a long poem–to be able to sustain the intensity of language and continue to move the poem forward. Long poems often seem pretentious; Kinnell taught me that they don't have to be.

Deja Everything is funny, outrageous and surreal. From Hammer, I suddenly got American surrealism. For me, humor is the key, and Hammer's poems are hilarious. In poems like "Guide to Marine Mammals and Sentence Structure" ("*9. Sentence With 'Velcro' In It* / Old poisonous Juan had a fondness for Velcro.") and "A Thousand Miles Away, Andy Williams' Thoughts Merge With My Own," Hammer pokes fun at the absurdities of our daily lives. He also created characters "Karl and Tina" who show up in more than one poem, and the use of recurring characters in poetry is something that I have explored in my own work. I have written a series of poems about "The Tenured Guy," a hapless academic, and those poems seem linked to the humorous pseudo-hippie-esque mysticism of Karl and Tina. The other thing Hammer's work did for me was help me see how references to popular culture could be used in poetry without sacrificing clarity. I think he was able to do this because of the wide range of references–it kept the poems from seeming too insider, or elitist. If you didn't know who Andy Williams was, you might know who Willie Mays was. He taught me that embracing aspect of poetry, even if he seemed to be giving rabbit ears to everyone while he embraced them.

Guillevic's *Euclidians* is an entire book of poems in response to various geometrical shapes, from "Straight Line" to "Dot," from "Cube" to "Rhomboid." Here, in its entirety, is "Sphere: 2":

> And what if there were
>
> only the two of us to carry on.

Along with each title is a drawing of the shape the poem refers to. For this poem, the drawing is of two circles that will always be separated.

Sometimes we come across books entirely by chance–I have no memory of how this book came into my possession, but I'm certainly glad I have it. *Euclidians* helped me write about very small things–subjects that might not seem capable of inspiring poetry. It also began the exploration of other art forms in my poetry. I have written a series of poems in response to Francis Bacon paintings, collaborated with a photographer (writing poems to go with her images), and written a series of poems designed to resemble the shape of a brick wall. All of these experiments owe something to Guillevic. The tension between the visual and the written word is there in every one of his deceptively simple poems. I strive always to be deceptively simple. There *is* poetry in a dot.

Miller Williams writes in his introduction to Parra's *Emergency Poems*, "Part of what is remarkable about Nicanor Parra's poetry is the sense it carries of the common, the everyday. We look at it and we almost say, 'Hell, anybody could have written that; these are just simple statements.' But we know no one else could have written them–that's how simple they are."

I can't articulate any better than that what I admire about Parra's work. Again, deceptive simplicity–something I strive hard to achieve in my own work. I also like the playfulness and absurdity of his poems:

> I would rather sleep in the open
> Than share
> A marriage bed with a turtle.

So often it is one word that changes everything. Like turtle. Or the juxtaposition of words in "Cathedrals really grab me by the balls." Or, the juxtaposition of lines. Yes, the language of each sentence is ordinary. But Parra is able to place two ordinary things next to each other and create the extraordinary. In "Well Then":

> don't be confused
> if you see me in two cities
> at once
> hearing mass in a chapel of the Kremlin
> or eating a hot dog
> in a New York airport

For me, that's it! To be in more than one place at the same time–very different places. And not to choke on the hot dog.

There you have it. Nine books—two novels, an anthology, and six books of poems. I have resisted the temptation to add a tenth book. I want to leave things open—to leave room for something new. In one way or another, that's what all these books have taught me.

DENISE DUHAMEL

Ai, *Cruelty*
Bill Knott, *Becos*
Sharon Olds, *Satan Says*
James Tate, *The Lost Pilot*
Stevie Smith, *Collected Poems*
Dylan Thomas, *Collected Poems*

I picked the six books that were most important to me very early on, when I first "knew" I wanted to become not only a writer, but a poet.

I suspect that Olds' first book, *Satan Says*, is on many poets' short lists of essential books. For me, this book gave me permission, more than any other, when it came to subject matter. Olds' bravery at tackling the taboo continues to astound and humble me.

The Lost Pilot, also a first book, dealt with very difficult raw material and I'm still very moved by the title poem. In addition, Tate's surreal bent in such poems as "Epithalamion for Tyler" which contains the lines "you go to the stockyards // buy a pig's ear and sew / it on the couch..." appealed to me as well. He could be rooted and "out there" at once, in the same book–sometimes in the same poem.

One of my favorite poems of all time (and one I find to be the most heartbreaking) is "The Closet," by Bill Knott, which is found in his book *Becos*. Like Olds and Tate, Knott also was dealing with extremely difficult subject matter–the death of his mother through the eyes of a young boy. The closet, empty of his mother's clothes, is full of hangers and the speaker jumps "Gropelessly to catch them to twist them clear, / Mis-shape them whole, sail them across the small air / Space of the closet..." Looking back, I was mesmerized by the way poets could transform the horrors of life and make something beautiful of them.

Nearly twenty years after first reading Ai's poem, "Child Beater," I still teach the poem almost every semester. The narrator in the poem is the child beater and the narrative is especially chilling. It's another way to get, again, to difficult subject matter–by speaking not from the victim's point of view, but instead the perpetrator's, thus, visiting the dark side. Ai manages more empathy for the battered child in this poem than if it were written in the child's voice.

Stevie Smith and Dylan Thomas were both very important to me in terms of word play, humor, and verve.

STEPHEN DUNN

Theodore Roethke, *Words for the Wind*
Wallace Stevens, *The Collected Poems*
James Dickey, *Poems: 1957-1967*
William Carlos Williams, *Selected Poems*
James Wright, *The Branch Will Not Break*

There are more, of course, but these books were important to me when I started to read and write poetry seriously in the late sixties.

Roethke's *Words for the Wind* for the combination of its music, sensuality, playfulness, and evocation of a psyche through natural imagery.

Stevens' *Collected Poems* was the only book of poems that I took with me to Spain, where I went to write a novel in 1967 and found out that my skills were better suited to poetry (I read Stevens that year pre-cognitively, happy to be among his imagination and his music).

Dickey's *Poems*, and especially his poem "The Sheep Child," taught me that, if you're good enough, anything is possible in poetry.

William Carlos Williams' *Selected Poems* for their sense of line and attention to the small, local things of the world.

And Wright's *The Branch Will Not Break* because it showed me a new way of speaking in a poem, a diction that was both colloquial and graceful and, finally, brilliantly tonal. It was a book that gave many of us significant permission to write a way that we thought could be peculiarly ours.

RUSSELL EDSON

Thank you for asking me to list 5-10 *essential titles*. I'm flattered that you might think my recommendations have any value...

While the development of the printing press (movable type and all) and the coming of the mass produced book is of historic interest; having myself read a number of these literary products, I am, alas, not able to recommend one 16th of an *essential title*, let alone one complete book.

The problem of most, if not all books, is the paradox of their words; thousands and thousands of them based on only 26 letters; these repeated and repeated in various combinations, making one tedious mass of words called a book. And that's the problem of the book, its abundance of words, which after a time seem only swarms of insects on its pages, hardly worth their sorting into words.

This is not to say that the uninitiated shouldn't try their hands at reading. By all means, no one in his heart of hearts wants to die a virgin.

Speaking to this, earlier on I might have recommended the works of Horatio Alger, Jr. Certainly a worthy writer, no one would dispute his gift. But his message, from the humble to the material achievement, seemed, finally after many readings, to champion an optimism life rarely earns. Albeit his books being the early models for my own psychological "Struggling Upward," as it were; my inspiration for even wanting to write.

Even today I would recommend Alger to the uninitiated as a first book-reading experience to let him or her discover what this reading business is all about, and to make a choice about continuing the activity, if only, as I've said, not to die a virgin. Even though these days I am psychologically drawn to avoid streets housing bookstores – the very thought of 26 letters repeated into millions of words jammed, choking in little shops is to wonder, if indeed, the Gutenberg thing (movable type and all) hasn't been overdone beyond even Johann's most extravagant dream?

But please understand, though I am mostly done with books, reading is not to be denied. The ability to write and read *talking* is a useful and remarkable tool for the keeping of records and the handling of information, such as road signs and gender clues on the doors of public toilets.

ELAINE EQUI

Federico García Lorca, *The Selected Poems*, ed. Francisco
    García Lorca and Donald Allen
The Random House Book of Twentieth-Century French Poetry, ed.
    Paul Auster
7 Greeks, trans. Guy Davenport
Technicians of the Sacred: A Range of Poetries from Africa, America,
    Asia, Europe and Oceania, ed. Jerome Rothenberg
From the Country of Eight Islands: An Anthology of Japanese Poetry,
    ed. and trans. Hiroaki Sato and Burton Watson
Laughing Lost in the Mountains: Poems of Wang Wei, trans. Tony
    Barnstone, Willis Barnstone and Xu Haixin
Proensa: An Anthology of Troubadour Poetry, trans. Paul Blackburn
Lorine Niedecker, *Collected Works*, ed. Jenny Penberthy
Frank O'Hara, *The Collected Poems*, ed. Donald Allen
Paul Celan, *Poems*, ed. and trans. Michael Hamburger

These are my all time favorite classics! They take me traveling
through time and space across poetic terrains ranging from shamanic
Eskimo visions, to fragments of Greek lyrics from the 7th century B.C.,
to the nature poems of the T'ang dynasty, to the cansos of 12th century
Provance, up to and including work from 20th century America, France,
and Spain.

Of course, the books here represent my own interests, particularly in
surrealism. I'm also, as you might guess from this list, partial to highly
concentrated forms such as haiku, aphorisms, proverbs, and epigrams.
Invaluable tools for anyone looking to pare down their writing and make
every word count would be found in Guy Davenport's *7 Greeks*, *From
the Country of Eight Islands*, Wang Wei, Lorine Niedecker and Paul
Celan.

Wherever else I might be led, the ideas in these books form a
constellation, almost a horoscope, of influences that have shaped my poetry.
They've helped me enormously and I pass them along confident that
they will have something inspiring to say to you too.

CLAYTON ESHLEMAN

~~~~~~~

Bud Powell, "Tea for Two"
Hart Crane, *The Collected Poems*
César Vallejo, *The Complete Posthumous Poetry*
William Blake, *The Complete Writings*
Origin magazine, ed. Cid Corman
Bashō, *Back Roads to Far Towns*, trans. Cid Corman and
     Kamaike Susumu
Chaïm Soutine's Impact
Wilhelm Reich, *The Function of the Orgasm*
Mikhail Bakhtin, *Rabelais and His World*

NINE FIRE SOURCES

On the morning of July 20, 1965, at the University of California Poetry Conference at Berkeley, Robert Duncan introduced Charles Olson's lecture, *Causal Mythology*. After mentioning several living poets he felt compelled to study–Pound, Zukofsky, Olson, Creeley, and Levertov- Duncan remarked:

> I return to find secrets, I return to *rob* them, you know. If I had
> to steal fire I know where to go, and there isn't any doubt.
> Everywhere else I might be stealing anything. I am a jackdaw
> in poetry. But I know when I'm coming home with a piece
> of colored glass that I've found that fits the design, and
> where to go for the fire at the center of things. For all of the
> poets who matter to me in my generation Charles Olson has
> been a Big Fire Source. One of the ones we have to study.

We are all jackdaws to varying degrees, and Duncan was one of the first to proudly acknowledge such. And the evocation of Prometheus, and the poet as the thief of fire, is also accurate, and timely. However, I believe that originality is still possible in art, including poetry. Those who openly acknowledge their plunder, as Duncan did, surely have tricks up their sleeves: behind such humble acknowledgements of being beholden to X or Y is a sense of poetic character convinced of the uniqueness of its expression.

Here are 9 of my fire sources. They focus on the formidable imaginations I discovered soon after discovering poetry in the late 1950s at Indiana University and my subsequent apprenticeship to the art in Kyoto in the early 1960s. This compilation can be read as an addenda to "Novices: A Study of Poetic Apprenticeship," collected in *Companion Spider* (Wesleyan University Press, 2002).

"Tea for Two," by Bud Powell

I started glancing at *Downbeat* magazine, around 1951, when I was 16. I taped two quarters to an order form and mailed it off, for a 45 RPM recording, with Lennie Tristano's "I Surrender, Dear" on the other side.

Piano as an orchestra of sound waterfalling through "Tea for Two" changes, with the skeleton of the melody baring its trivia from moment to moment. I listened to it again and again, trying to grasp the difference between the song line and what Powell was doing to it. Melody versus improvisation, what someone else had written versus what Powell was doing to and with it. Somehow an idea vaguely made its way through: you don't have to play somebody else's melody–you can improvise (how?), make up your own tune! WOW–really? You mean, I don't have to be my parents? I don't have to "play their melody" for the rest of my life?

The alternative–being myself–was a stupendous enigma that took me another 6 years to even begin to approach. I had to get completely bored with all the possibilities my given life had prepared me for (including playing the piano) before I could make a grab at something that challenged me to change my life.

Later I realized that Powell had taken the trivial in music (as Art Tatum did with "I'll See You in My Dreams") and transformed it into an imaginative structure. William Carlos Williams, I noted, had done something similar in poetry.

While reading the Sunday Comics on the living-room floor was probably my first encounter, as a boy, with imagination, Powell was my first encounter, as an adolescent, with the figure of the artist.

In *The Gull Wall* (1975), I wrote a poem which brooded about Powell's tragic life and about what he had offered me, which, in the writing of the poem, seemed to cut all the way back to the neighborhood piano teacher lessons my mother started me on at 6:

> Bud Powell
> locked in his Paris bathroom so he wouldn't wander.
> Sipping his lunch from the cat
> saucer on the floor.
> I see him curled there, nursing his litter,
> his great swollen dugs,
> his sleepy Buddha face

looks down through the lotus pond,
sees the damned, astral miles below,
amongst them a little unmoving Clayton Jr.,
placed by his mother on a bed of keys.
Powell compassionately extended his tongue,
licked my laid out senses.

The Collected Poems of Hart Crane

I bought a copy of the 1933 edition in Robert Wilson's Phoenix Bookstore, NYC, 1960, on the same trip in from Indiana during which I met Robert Kelly, Jerry Rothenberg, and Paul Blackburn. Like Pablo Neruda, Crane brought home metaphor to me, but on a more complex, concentrated, and challenging level than the sensuous, Surreal Chilean. At first, I went for the "easy" poems in *White Buildings*, like "My Grandmother's Love Letters," with its "loose girdle of soft rain," and paper "brown and soft ... liable to melt as snow." Then I became amazed with the unexpected juxtapositions in Crane, such as one finds in the first stanza of "Praise for an Urn":

> It was a kind and northern face
> That mingled in such exile guise
> The everlasting eyes of Pierrot
> And, of Gargantua, the laughter.

The placement of "Gargantua" before "laughter" taught me something about balancing a line. And to find "the crematory lobby" in the 4th stanza suddenly contextualized "urn" and made the poem poignantly real. Small matters, perhaps, but "divine particulars," or building blocks, for a poetry in which every word must count.

Poems like "Lachrymae Christi" and "The Wine Menagerie" stopped me in my tracks in the same way that some of Blake did. I was being asked to stretch to accommodate an uncommon sense of things that I was intuitively convinced was not nonsense or pointlessly obscure. Crane invented a term, "the logic of metaphor," to identify the way metaphor can lead to metaphor and create a narrative that is utterly imaginative. His metaphoric shifts recall chord changes in bebop, or strokes in a De Kooning painting of the 1960s. Reading Crane is like watching colored fragments in a turned kaleidoscope slip into new symmetries, then rearrange again.

Over the years, Hart Crane has become a poet companion and from time to time I am moved to either address him in a poem or to project his addressing me. On one hand, he is a tragic auto-didact who never learned self-regulation and destroyed himself, on one level, in revenge against those who would not acknowledge and support his genius. On the other hand, at his best, Crane is the most original American poet of the 20th century. Had he been able to deal with his new-found relationship with Peggy Baird in Mexico in 1931, he might have been able to derail his masochistic homosexuality. In such poems, written near the end of his life, such as "The Circumstance" and "Havana Rose," a voice freed of traditional verse emerges. However, I think it is only fair to acknowledge that the forces that drove him to destroy himself also at certain points released his imagination.

No poet to my knowledge has ever speared memory as Crane did in "Passages":

> Sulking, sanctioning the sun,
> My memory I left in a ravine, –
> Casual louse that tissues the buckwheat,
> Aprons rocks, congregates pears
> In moonlit bushels
> And wakens alleys with a hidden cough.

I have never forgotten for a moment the last two lines of the third section of "Voyages":

> The imagination spans beyond despair,
> Outpacing bargain, vocable and prayer.

César Vallejo, *The Complete Posthumous Poetry*

César Vallejo (1892-1938) published his second and revolutionary book, *Trilce*, in 1922. As the poet himself later put it, the book fell into a void–no response, no reviews. Peruvian readers may have received *Trilce* with the same sort of bafflement with which American readers would have received 100 pages of non-bowdlerized Emily Dickinson in the mid-1860s. Both poets had cleared new grounds in consciousness that put them beyond the sensibilities of their times.

I discovered Vallejo's poetry while a student at Indiana University in the late 1950s and determined, in Kyoto, 1962, to translate *Poemas humanos* as my apprenticeship to poetry. By 1964, I had realized that because all editions of these poems contained errors, I had to inspect the worksheets that were in the possession of Vallejo's widow, Georgette. With $300 and my pregnant first wife, I arrived in Lima in the fall of 1965. Not only did Georgette refuse to show me the worksheets, she refused me permission to publish my versions on the basis that Vallejo was untranslatable (this while she completed a translation of a selected poems in French). After I returned to the states in the summer of 1966, a friend of mine in Lima tricked her into signing a homemade contract. Grove Press decided that it would stand up in court, and brought out *Human Poems* in 1968. A few years later, in Los Angeles, I showed my translation to José Rubia Barcia, a Spanish scholar and essayist teaching at UCLA. He said that while it was not bad, it could be improved, so together we redid the whole collection, at this point with access to the worksheets which had been privately-published in Lima. José's and my co-translation was published by University of California Press in 1978 as *César Vallejo: The Complete Posthumous Poetry.*

I have thought more about poetry while translating Vallejo than while reading anyone else, and if my own work has been influenced by him, such influence is indirect: via what I have turned him into in English. He taught me that contradiction is an aspect of metaphor and gave me permission to try anything in my quest for an authentic alternative world in poetry.

If Vallejo is one model for American poets today, as Eliot Weinberger has recently remarked, I think that his usefulness has little to do with writing political poetry–by which I mean poetry with a cause to advance. I think that the key Vallejo lesson may lie in a poet learning how to become imprisoned, as it were, in global life as a whole, and in each moment in particular. Some of the homework for such a position, for an American poet especially, involves learning what our government has been doing in the world for the past 60 years and to grasp the amount of pain we have caused others (as well as many of our own citizens). Vallejo's European poetry urges the poet to confront his own destiny and to stew in what is happening to him and also to believe that his bewildering situation is significant. To face one's own destiny is to know that not only is one finite but that the world one lives in is becoming more disposable by the hour and that no conceivable political revolution could make a significant difference. To be bound to, or imprisoned in, the present, includes confronting not only life as it really is but psyche as it really is not–weighing all affirmation against our imperial obsessions and one's own intrinsic dark.

The Complete Writings of William Blake

I purchased the Nonesuch Press edition in Kyoto, February 1963, and a few months later scribbled on the title page: "*The Four Zoas, Milton*, and *Jerusalem* in 1963 can be read as the Bible in 1863; the Bible still makes sense but has lost energy in time." I suppose I was attempting to say that Blake's "Prophetic Books" were, for our era, the book of life.

When I wasn't translating Vallejo in those days, I mostly tried to read all of Blake. His work hit me in gusts, and putting it all together–holding "Milton" say, as a single work, in mind–was impossible. So I read Northrop Frye's *Fearful Symmetry* to discover it was as difficult, in its own way, as Blake himself! I discovered a used facsimile edition of *The First Book of Urizen* in a bookstore, and while reading it one afternoon, I passed out, to wake up an hour or so later, flat on the tatami, the book still in my hand.

Blake is the most bold of poets, and possessed of a confidence powerful enough to keep him at his work while facing humiliating neglect. Who else might have written:

> I have travel'd tho' Perils & Darkness not unlike a Champion.
> I have conquer'd, and shall still Go on Conquering. Nothing
> can withstand the fury of my Course among the Stars of God &
> in the Abysses of the Accuser.

Or:

> To cleanse the Face of my Spirit by Self-examination,
> To bathe in the Waters of Life, to wash off the Not Human,
> I come in Self-annihilation & the grandeur of Inspiration,
> To cast off Rational Demonstration by Faith in the Savior,
> To cast off the rotten rags of Memory by Inspiration,
> To cast off Bacon, Locke & Newton from Albion's covering,
> To take off his filthy garments & clothe him with Imagination,
> To cast aside from Poetry all that is not Inspiration...

Blake is also very insightful, especially as a young writer when his thought was not entangled, as it was in his later years, with accommodating the Christian system. I doubt if anyone else alive in his London of the late 18th century had the following thoughts regarding feminine sexuality and what men had made of it:

> Murder is Hindering Another. Theft is Hindering Another.
> Backbiting, Undermining, Circumventing, & whatever is
> Negative is Vice. But the origin of this mistake in Lavater &
> his cotemporaries is, They suppose that Woman's Love is Sin;
> in consequence all the Loves & Graces with them are Sins.

And:

> What is it men in women do require?
> The lineaments of Gratified Desire.

What is it women in men require?
The lineaments of Gratified Desire.

Reciprocity, I discovered via Blake, is the daily, human goal.

Origin magazine, second series (1961-1964), edited by Cid Corman

In Kyoto, 1962, once a week I would walk downtown from the Japanese house my first wife and I shared with a family to The Muse Coffeeshop, to spend the evening with Cid Corman. Since Cid lived alone in a small room, he had turned The Muse into an office of sorts, where he read, edited, and translated. Anyone who wanted to talk with him knew to find him there.

For about two years, I learned the rudiments of literary magazine editing and translating from Cid. I waited eagerly for each issue of *Origin*, a quarterly, to appear, and having introjected its editor as an aesthetic censor got into arguments with myself over the difference between what *Origin* proposed and what I was trying to write. For much of these two years I lived in a multiple vise, caught between Corman, Vallejo whom I was   trying to translate, and an overwhelming first reading of all of Blake. I was in that self-confrontational limbo, where many novice poets quit. Squatting in the benjo one morning I realized that I was in a similar position to Tlatzeotl-Ixcuina, the Aztec goddess of filth and childbirth, a stone carving with a tiny god-infant projecting between her thighs. I too wanted to give birth but all that seemed to come out of me was shit.

Origin, second series, consisted of 14 issues, each 64 pages. The magazine's motto was: "to respond   to offer   to let be" (Corman's "translation" of T. S. Eliot's "to give, to sympathize, to control"). The magazine was free–if you wrote and asked for it. The author focus of the second series was Zukofsky's *"A"* and his co-translations of Catullus. Zukofsky was also involved in the magazine's ending after the 14th issue, instead of the intended 20. My memory is that he told Cid he would be better off doing something else.

Each issue was composed in a way that few literary magazines are. One work often sounded another, and there was a cogent fabric of shorter and longer pieces. Here are some of the works from this series that I studied carefully and took to heart as one trying to find his way in poetry:

Sections from Gary Snyder's *Mountains and Rivers Without End*, #2, 4, and 12.
"Yashima," a Noh play by Zeami, #3.
Robert Kelly 's "The Exchanges," #5.

Michael McClure's "The Held Back Pain," #6.
Twenty-four Poems by Rocco Scotellaro, #7.
"A letter, of sorts," by Gael Turnbull, #7.
Giacomo Leopardi's "L' Infinito," #8.
Cid Corman's "The Contingency," #8.
Seven Poems by Eugenio Montale, #9.
Excerpts from "The Day Book" by Robert Duncan, #10.
René Char's "The Lace of Montmirail," #11.
Jean-Paul de Dadelsen's "Bach in Autumn," #11.
Bashō's "Oku-no-hosomichi," #14.

Origin, second series, was like having a seminar with all the figures mentioned above, and my introduction to what Robert Duncan would, a few years later, identify as a "symposium of the whole." A great deal of what appeared in this series of *Origin* still holds up for me, as vital and lively. I take this as a testament to Cid Corman's dedication and acuity as a poet/translator/editor.

<u>Bashō'*s Back Roads to Far Towns*</u>

The Cid Corman/Kamaike Susumu translation of Bashō's last and most impressive hike journal (in which poet and companion walked some 1500 miles) was published in *Origin* magazine, July, 1964, under the Japanese title: *Oku-no-hosomichi*. It was published as a book by Mushinsha-Grossman in 1968. To the best that I can tell, it is the finest translation of haiku (and haibun, which is prose accompanying haiku) that has ever been done in English.

Wallace Stevens once wrote, in *Adagia*, that "Poetry is the scholar's art." As I read it, he means that poetry is the literary art that should hold the greatest appeal to scholars. Poets can also be scholars without lessening the intuitive drive it takes to write substantial poetry. Bashō is a sterling example of the spiritual poet/scholar. He did his homework on the lore and history concerning the sites and temples he planned to visit on his three long hikes. The narrative drift of his haibun is like a parachute weighted with a haiku body under it. Or to put it another way: it is a pleasure to visit and describe precisely what one has seen (haibun); it is more challenging, after, to sense the essence of the seen, to sound it in the tiny crucible of a haiku. Here is Bashō's May 27th entry, haibun followed by haiku:

In the demesne of Yamagata the mountain temple called Ryushakuji. Founded by Jikaku Daishi, unusually well-kept place. "You must go and see it," people urged; from here, off back towards Obanazawa, about seven li. Sun not yet down. Reserved space at dormitory at bottom, then climbed to temple on ridge. This mountain one of rocky steeps, ancient pines and cypresses, old earth and stone and smooth moss, and on the rock temple-doors locked, no sound. Climbed along edges of and crept over boulders, worshipped at temples, penetrating scene, profound quietness, heart/mind open clear.

> quiet
> into rock absorbing
> cicada sounds

Chaïm Soutine's Impact

I saw my first Soutine in 1963 in the Ohara Museum of Art, Kurashiki, Japan, "Hanging Duck," painted in Paris around 1925. Seeing this painting was so riveting that I recall nothing else in the museum. It was a hybrid fusion, at once a flayed man hung from a pulpy wrist and flailing, with gorgeous white wings attached to his leg stumps–and a gem-like putrescent bird, snagged by one leg, in an underworld filled with bird-beaked monsters and zooming gushes of blood-color and sky-blue paint. For some forty years I have kept Soutine's art in heart and mind.

In 1993, Maurice Tuchman, Esti Dunow, and Klaus Peris edited *Chaïm Soutine* (1893-1943) *Catalogue Raisonné* (Benedikt Taschen Verlag, Cologne), a boxed two-volume collection of some 800 pages. A magnificent advance on all Soutine books and catalogues up to then, it included newly-discovered paintings (and rejected some mediocre pieces, which had been used over the years to criticize Soutine's standing, as fakes). I celebrated devouring this collection by writing a 22 page poem, "Soutine's Lapis" (collected in *From Scratch*, Black Sparrow Press, 1998).

In "Another Way of Seeing," an essay in the March 2002 *Harper's Magazine*, John Berger writes: "More directly than any other art, painting is an affirmation of the existent, of the physical world into which mankind has been thrown." Soutine always worked from a model, whether it was a bunch of houses in a hillscape, a beef carcass, or a human being. Like Caravaggio, he never (with two exceptions) drew. His "existents"–especially when he was in Céret, France (1919-22)–besides being his focus, are also projection-spooked. Whatever Soutine looked at in Céret seems to have pulled wads of childhood nightmare out of him. These landscapes are not only in earthquake rumba mode, but are pixilated with a very personal, anthropomorphic hysteria. Houses often have grotesque expressions – something between a house and a terrified human face. Some houses even twist into humanesque shapes – they cower in clumps like frightened children or crawl up onto the "backs" of their neighbors.

Céret is strangely enough Soutine's extreme point (thinking of Vallejo for a moment, it is his *Trilce*). Had he been willing to abandon his "existents," he might have become an abstract expressionist (De Kooning called him his "favorite artist"). But he recoiled from his work at Céret – later destroying a significant amount of it – and his post-Céret work (1923-1943) is a kind of crabwise retreat into traditional painting. To put it this way is a little misleading because some of the later portraits, the beef carcasses, most of the hanging fowl, the rayfish, and some of the last landscapes at Civry and Champigny are wonderful, bold achievements – yet none are as audacious or as intuitively fearless as the Céret work. It is as if John Coltrane played free form jazz as a young musician and then, after a few years, improvised off standards for the rest of his life.

In the fall of 1999, my wife Caryl and I visited Céret. We went to the museum, had lunch, and walked around for a while trying to get some sense of what Céret might have been when Soutine was there 80 years before. Finding little of the painter's presence in the town, we got in our car and started to drive away. Halfway out of town, I spotted an ancient bridge and impulsively stopped the car. I asked Caryl to wait there while I walked up onto the bridge and wrote down some notes:

> Standing on Céret's 14th century Pont de diable, a Neanderthal brow-bridge over muddy, cascading water spiking the shores. Funnel-shaped drifting smoke, plumes of mauve going null brown. At 3 PM, at the end of Soutine's century. Sky and river full of Chaïm, the whole studio bobbing along. Frames, rams, anti-ams. Chicken-neck twisting river. As if through a beef carcass basin, the auburn water boils.

> Hanging on museum walls: the husks of chrysalis-split moment, nettle shirts of transmuted hurt.

> Like Soutine, I inserted myself, a splinter, an anti-fixation, churning to get loose – and
> I am still in havoc with those I love, still
> at the granite dissidence that
> bids me to write.

At the poet Joel Oppenheimer's wedding party at Max's Kansas City bar and restaurant, NYC, July of 1966, I started dancing with a woman named Adrienne, and by the end of that evening I was wildly infatuated with her. I decided to leave my wife and infant son and to follow out wherever a relationship with Adrienne would take me. She had recently completed therapy with Alexander Lowen; during the therapy she had left her photographer husband, and when I met her she was hiding out from him, with their two children, behind a steel-doored apartment on the Lower East Side. Connecting with Adrienne threw me into a black quandary: why had it taken me five years to realize that my first wife was not the person I really wanted to be with? Impressed by the effect of therapy on Adrienne, I made an appointment with Lowen. Neither of us liked each other. So I asked Adrienne: who did Lowen study with? Who was *his* mentor? Before leaving for a vacation in Greece with her children, Adrienne handed me her copy of Wilhelm Reich's *The Function of the Orgasm*.

I sat down in the basement room on Bank Street I had moved into and started reading the Reich book. Halfway through, I got up, packed a bag, made a plane reservation, flew back to Indianapolis, took a cab to my childhood home and informed my mother that I had to talk with her. I told her that we had never had an honest conversation and that I did not love her like she thought I did. I was trying to declare independence and make a final break with Indiana. My mother, of course, was simply bewildered and hurt. After our talk, I disappeared into the basement and tried to come to terms with what I had just done. I scribbled into a notebook:

> Today I have set my crowbar against all I know
> In a shower of blood and soot
> Breaking the backbone of my mother.
> > 11 September 1966

Then, sick with remorse for having done what I had felt compelled to do, I wrote "The 1802 Blake Butts Letter Variation," in which I acknowledged that I had put knowledge over love, and had broken a heart "to save my own destruction."

In *The Function of the Orgasm*, Reich argued that the goal of individual life was self-regulation, and that the "function of the orgasm," was to enable the individual to become self-regulative and creatively responsive. For Reich there was no contradiction between sexual fulfillment and imaginative realization – they were antiphonal, mutually reinforcing. Reich's position hit me like a thunderbolt: and it emboldened me to do something I had never done before: to cut through all obligation and to proclaim my right to live for myself alone, on the assumption that such was fundamental to do anything original as a poet. The downside of this personal revolution was my guilt for what I had first put my wife through, and then my mother.

I returned to NYC, went into Reichian therapy with Dr. Sidney Handelman, and began to decompress years of stifled feelings and self-thwarted stances. My goal was to come to terms with why I had put obligation over action. Using Reich as my sounding board, I felt like, in Wallace Stevens' words, "the latest freed man." I was soon to discover that abusive honesty is part of the wake of release.

Rabelais and His World by Mikhail Bakhtin

An old friend, the cook-book writer and Classics scholar, Denis Kelly, gave me Bakhtin' s book, the summer of 1973, not long after my book *Coils* was published. In Coils I had attempted to excavate my Indiana background and to lay bare the stances that I felt diminished humanness. Inspired by Blake's invented mythic world, I created my own god-forms to help me free myself to explore the irrational. I revealed myself more than my rationality would accept, and when the book was published I felt that I was alone and in water over my head.

While many poets attempt to be original in one way or another, it is also gratifying to discover that one's own efforts to clear new ground have some antecedent support – that another thinker has established a background against which one's own efforts can be viewed and contextualized. Bakhtin's vision of "grotesque realism," cogently presented in the 60 page Introduction to *Rabelais and His World*, not only backed up my own ambivalence toward the human body but proposed an "archaic grotesque" that helped me gain a perspective on Ice Age imagery, which I discovered the following year after Caryl and I had taken up residence for several months in the French Dordogne. Bakhtin's book helped me negotiate the transformation involved with turning away from my personal background and facing the most impersonal background imaginable: materials without historical frame or recorded language.

Via Rabelais' book of laughter, fearlessness, and transformation, the Russian Bakhtin brought across a vision of man returning unto himself, with destruction but an aspect of regeneration and renewal. Such continues to inspire me, especially as I face negations in the 20th and 21st centuries that are of such a scale as to often render any affirmation a Gargantuan dream.

B. H. FAIRCHILD

Ernest Thompson Seton, *Biography of a Grizzly*
King James Bible
Herman Melville, *Moby Dick*
Fyodor Dostoevsky, *The Brothers Karamazov*
The Short Stories of Ernest Hemingway
Anthony Hecht, *The Hard Hours*
William Shakespeare, *Hamlet*
Jan Zwicky, *Lyric Philosophy*
John Keats, *Poems*
James Agee, *A Death in the Family*

We use the phrase, "It changed my life," rather too easily these days, but I think that *Biography of a Grizzly*, read when I was a boy of ten, actually did that. Arriving at the last unforgettable page of this story, when the old bear goes into the last canyon, where he knows he will die, I came to understand something about nobility and dignity and the Greek sense of tragedy long before I had words for those things. I have written of it elsewhere: "I cannot forget the exhilaration I felt at the time, the centripetal pull of the words, the feeling that I was at the center of something, that between myself and the words on the page was a world bearing significance and authenticity, a world that somehow existed not outside but within the other one."

Though as a child I did not enjoy attending church, I know that the syntax and rhythms of the King James translation were music to me even then, and still flow through me, as they have through so many writers of English.

I read both *Moby Dick* and *The Brothers Karamazov* during my sophomore year of college, and I may as well have been reading the secrets of the cosmos or *Life: Its Meaning and Mystery*. I walked around in a sort of intellectual daze followed by a hunger that has never left me and has filled my house with far too many books.

I read many of Hemingway's short stories in high school, becoming vaguely aware for the first time of the thing called prose style, that a writer was doing something entirely unique and beautiful with the English sentence.

Hecht's *The Hard Hours* is one of the great books of American poetry. As an example of what wondrous things could be done with the language in my own time, it has sustained me through moments of cultural despair.

Hamlet was the first Shakespeare play where I felt that I had really gotten "inside" the language and therefore inside Shakespeare's genius.

I encountered Zwicky's strange, brilliant book five or six years ago, and it's the kind of catalyzing and clarifying work that I know for the remainder of my writing years I will not only be rereading but meditating upon, dwelling in, *living with*.

Keats' *Poems*, with Shakespeare, is my main source of examples of the auditory imagination at the highest level.

I could put any of about twenty novels in this spot, but Agee's *A Death in the Family* seemed to have been written in the most exactingly crafted prose about my experience in the world, my people, and somehow my own interior life.

ANNIE FINCH

Christopher Alexander, *The Timeless Way of Building*
Hart Crane, *Collected Poems*
Emily Dickinson, *Complete Poems*
Gyorgi Doczi, *The Power of Limits*
Anne Finch, Countess of Winchilsea, *Collected Poems*
Audre Lorde, *The Black Unicorn*
Edna St. Vincent Millay, *Collected Sonnets*
Frank O'Hara, *Complete Poems*
Edmund Spenser, *Complete Poems*
Merlin Stone, *When God Was a Woman*
Sweet's Anglo-Saxon Primer
John Thompson, *The Founding of English Meter*
Lao Tzu, *Tao Te Ching*
Oscar Williams, *Immortal Poems of the English Language*

The Timeless Way of Building, Alexander's book on architecture, reassured me about the importance of a whole set of values that has infused my poetry: human scale, a certain level of physical and rhythmic accessibility, strength and harmony of proportion, cultural sustainability, and a paradoxical trust in simplicity. Doczi's classic *Power of Limits* helped me trace a wider spiritual context for my aesthetic convictions.

Merlin Stone's work opened me to a whole area of thought based in female-centered spirituality, Wicca, and ecopsychology, which proved essential to my growth as an earth-centered and spiritual poet. Lao Tzu is the best guide I know for actual writing practice.

I almost didn't include any books of poetry, since the number of books of poetry that have been essential to me as a poet is so immense that any choice is vexed. My list could also have included Homer, Herbert, Keats, Osgood, Swinburne, Lawrence, Yeats, Frost, Teasdale, Plath, Hughes, Brooks, Sanchez, Auden, Tsvetaeva, Elytis, and numerous others.

At a crucial point, I carried Hart Crane's poems around for months; they gave me the courage to trust my verbal sensuality and my hermetic vision. The raw integrity of his art has always been a benchmark for my poems. Frank O'Hara showed me that I could maintain my innocence and still be a rebel. The simplicity of his voice and George Herbert's still serves as one aesthetic axis whenever I write and rewrite.

Sweet's Primer taught me to read Anglo-Saxon poetry and stands in here for *Beowulf* and Anglo-Saxon narrative poems and riddles, as well as Middle English poetry and Greek. All of these gave me a long sense of my poetry's context and permanently de-familiarized my language for me. John Thompson's *The Founding of English Meter* taught me the metaphysical importance of prosody and meter, teaching me that the mind/body paradox in poetry is exactly as much of a spiritual mystery as it is in life.

Lorde's *The Black Unicorn*, a talisman of a book that Lorde did not allow to be excerpted or anthologized, is a reminder to me always of how personal poetry is, how uncompromisingly individual is its spiritual work. Millay, whose sonnets my mother and sister used to recite for me, first gave me the idea that women can be important poets. Her poetry has worn well, reminding me that emotional experience in female-centered terms remains true poetic tender. I pretty much cohabitated with Williams' *Immortal Poems of the English Language* during my late childhood and early adolescence. These poems taught me how much cultural work a poem can do while providing accessible pleasure.

Spenser, Finch, and Dickinson are like my family members. Their lessons can't really be paraphrased; whether I ignore or make up with or quarrel with them, they are there.

ALICE FRIMAN

Gerard Manley Hopkins, *The Poems of Gerard Manley Hopkins*
Louise Glück, *The Wild Iris*
Louise Glück, *The Seven Ages*
Mary Oliver, *American Primitive*
David Bottoms, *Under the Vulture-Tree*
Derek Walcott, *Collected Poems*
Jorie Graham, *Materialism*
The Women's Encyclopedia of Myths and Secrets, ed. Barbara G. Walker
Roberto Calasso, *The Ruin of Kasch*
Roberto Calasso, *Ka*
Roberto Calasso, *The Marriage of Cadmus and Harmony*

To begin, I should begin at the beginning. Picture it, I was twenty-seven and vacuuming, when over the whine of the sweeper, I heard poems being read on the radio. I turned off the machine and listened. When it was over, I realized two things: first, I hadn't understood a word that had been said, and second, that whatever it was or whoever it was, it was incredible. The top of my head came off / I cut myself shaving–the true tests–whatever. I was hooked. I think the operable word here is *thrilling*. Many years later, after I had taught those very poems over and over again, I could still say they were thrilling. And I find them so now. I am talking, of course, about the poems of Gerard Manley Hopkins, not just his earlier ecstatic ones, but also the "terrible sonnets," including "Carrion Comfort," the one he said was "written in blood." Lest my enthusiasm be mistaken for some sort of religious affinity, let me say, "That is not it at all, / That is not what I meant, at all" (thank you, Tom). It is emotional power engendered by feelings held in check and held in check until it cannot help but burst forth. For me, reading Hopkins is like being struck by a geyser that has never lost its power to overwhelm. And that's what I want from poetry. I am not interested in work imitating paint drying on a wall. Or games. And because life is difficult, I take my poetry difficult. Is this turning into a rant? Okay, so my first choice would be *The Poems of Gerard Manley Hopkins*.

Who else? Louise Glück, especially the work in *The Wild Iris* and in *The Seven Ages* where the poems seem to be not only driven by a fierce intelligence but controlled by it to the extent that the emotion having nowhere to go must climb an intricate interior staircase looking for release. Out the attic window perhaps. In that way, she seems Hopkinsesque. Look at these lines at the end of "Stars," my favorite from *The Seven Ages*. The day is speaking, the "unsatisfying morning":

> Do you reject me? Do you mean
> to send me away because I am not
> full, in your word,
> because you see
> the black shape already implicit?
> I will never be banished. I am the light,
> your personal anguish and humiliation.
> Do you dare
> send me away as though
> you were waiting for something better?
>
> There is no better.
> Only (for a short space)
> the night sky like
> a quarantine that sets you
> apart from your task.
> Only (softly, fiercely)
> the stars shining. Here,
> in the room, the bedroom.
> Saying *I was brave, I resisted,*
> *I set myself on fire.*

It is that burst at the end I covet, that "where on earth did that come from" which, of course, was implicit all along. Is she an "influence" on me? I'd like to think so, perhaps if only in the way Everest defines the climber. Whatever it is, I'll take it.

I remember when Mary Oliver's *American Primitive* came out. Here was a collection that said, Look, poems exist all around you. Here in this book was the great permission: imagery and insight in plain speech racing down a page. Poems I've never gotten tired of.

Then there are the books that live on my desk and that I take with me to every colony or retreat: perhaps they are my totems. One that I've had an interesting relationship with over the years is David Bottoms' *Under the Vulture-Tree*. It used to belong to my husband until I confiscated it. Sometimes when I'd get stuck in a piece, writing myself into a corner, I'd open the book at random, shut my eyes and point. "Okay, David," I'd say, "show me how to do this." Mind you, I didn't know the man, but damned if the magic didn't work.

There are other books I use that way: Walcott's *Collected Poems*, Jorie Graham's *Materialism*, and *The Woman's Encyclopèdia of Myths and Secrets* to name a few. Then there are the *Field Guides*, of course; how can a writer do without them? Trees, birds, wild flowers, insects, etc.

But my ace in the hole is the three books I have by the Italian scholar Roberto Calasso: *The Ruin of Kasch*, *Ka*, and *The Marriage of Cadmus and Harmony*. More intriguing than Ovid, more intricate, imaginative, and just plain smarter than any sixty scholars you know, this man and his work are my constant companions. The books, inexhaustible.

AMY GERSTLER

Ok, here's one possible list out of hundreds I am tempted to draw up:

Sei Shonagon, *The Pillow Book of Sei Shonagon* (Ancient Japanese
poetic diary of sorts, but that pale description doesn't convey how
feisty, witty, observant, discerning, self possessed, endearingly
haughty and contemporary the prose is. Stuffed with amazing lists
like "Embarrassing Things," "Things that Give a Clean Feeling,"
"Adorable Things," "Squalid Things," etc.)
Franz Kafka, *The Complete Short Stories of Franz Kafka* (Fabulous
from cover to cover, it contains "The Country Doctor" one of the
strangest and most poetic short stories I've ever encountered.)
Virginia Woolf, *A Room of One's Own* or any of her collections of
essays or her novels or letters.
James Tate, *Selected Poems* or any of his books of poems.
MFK Fisher, *The Art of Eating* (Compendium of 5 shorter prose books,
memoir-istic in approach, about eating, cooking, being human,
love, memory, the senses. Auden once said she was, for his
money, the best prose writer in English.)
Evan S. Connell, *Mrs. Bridge* (Gem of a novel in tiny chapters by a
brilliant writer.)
Frank O'Hara, *The Selected Poems of Frank O'Hara*
Denis Johnson, *Jesus' Son* (Blow mind short stories.)
Elizabeth Bishop, *The Collected Poems*
Wislawa Szymborska. Any of her books of poems.

Yours truly is a cheater from way back. I will substantiate this
claim by immediately flouting the reasonable guidelines provided by the
respected editor of this volume. That is to say that I am going to bring
up other books in this brief statement, and not limit myself to mentioning only 5-10 as suggested. Please forgive me. I understand I may be
booted out of the anthology. But citing only ten books is like having a
10th or 30th or 50th birthday party and being told you can only invite two
people, if you are a very social sort and have lots and lots of dear, essential friends. Unfortunately, I'm not an especially social sort but have
always been a greedy and obsessed reader and it pains me to acknowledge only ten books as having aided and abetted me in writing and living. It makes me feel like an ingrate. So here's my cheater's list of
another 13 volumes:

Walt Whitman, *Leaves of Grass*

Benjamin Weissman, *Dear Dead Person* and *Headless* (Two intense,
   gorgeous, wild books of short stories by a guy who writes like a
   fusion of Kafka, Melville, and David Lynch and to whom I have
   the good fortune to be married.)
Sylvia Plath, *Collected Poems*
Tom Clark. Any of his books of poems.
Bert Meyers. Ditto. (Supposedly this sadly out of print author will
   soon have a collected poems available.)
Putnam's Complete Book of Quotations, Proverbs and Household Words
   (I'm a fiend for old reference books filled with beautiful quotes
   that date back to ancient Greece and Rome as well as cryptic
   folksy sayings from various times and places.)
Charles Simic. Any book of his poems.
Joe Brainard, *I Remember* (Unique, inspiring, easy to read book length
   autobiographical poem in short prose entries that you will never
   regret owning or having read.)
The Art of the Personal Essay, ed. Phillip Lopate. (Indispensable
   anthology that proves that poetry and essays are sister arts.)
Freud. (Sigmund was a rare, lively mind and writer. Many works are
   more accessible than you ever dreamed.)
The I Ching, trans. Richard Wilhelm
Joan Didion, *The White Album* or *Slouching Towards Bethlehem*
   (Classic American essays.)
Bernard Cooper, *Maps to Anywhere* (A unique book in which fiction,
   nonfiction, and poetry somehow perform a three way mating and
   have lovely offspring.)

   Now I feel criminal and a little ill for leaving out Rilke, Russell
Edson, Akhmatova, Baudelaire, Shakespeare, Lewis Carroll, Edward
Lear, Sharon Olds, Ai, Mark Twain, Amos Tutola, *The Story of the
Stone*, *Moby Dick*, Bruno Schulz, Ben Okri, *As I Lay Dying,* Elaine
Equi's poems, Lucia Perillo's poems, *The Anatomy of Melancholy*,
Barthelme's *Forty Stories*, *The Oxford Book of Essays*, Ian Stevenson's
books about reincarnation...Help! This is a disaster. All the unmentioned
books crammed into sagging shelves in this tiny room where I write
accuse me of neglect. Dusting them will not get me back in their good
graces, I'm afraid. I also fear I have defeated the commendable purpose
of this exercise in which we were to narrow our selections down to
under a dozen, an amount of books that could be carried to the car by
someone with strong biceps in one armload. While I take responsibility for
this transgression, I think a little of the blame must be placed on the
influence of uncountable essential books I am surrounded by (more

being written every day). I hope to spend a good portion of the rest of my life spreading the word about them. If I have spread it a little too thinly or thickly here, I'll try to pretend to act like I'm sorry.

ALBERT GOLDBARTH

Sven Birkerts, *The Gutenberg Elegies*
Lewis Hyde, *The Gift*
Lucretius, *On the Nature of the Universe*
Walter Murch, *In the Blink of An Eye*
Joseph J. Ellis, *After the Revolution*
Wendy Kaminer, *Sleeping With Extraterrestrials*

I think I'm constitutionally incapable of generating a list of books that have been "formative" to my own writing. That kind of self-scholarship (or self-analysis or self-archeology: call it what you will, this po' biz self-concern that exists outside of the body of the poems themselves) doesn't hold much attraction for me. Nor, frankly, do I think my "influences"–even if I *could* enumerate them–are anybody's business. Let my poems stand on their own, I say. And let everybody else's too. More than once I've had occasion to quote a statement of Peter Wild's: "It's the beer we're interested in, not the can."

Still, your solicitation seems filled with goodwill, and asks to be met half-way, even by someone with misgivings. I've presumed to spin your invitation around a bit, and I asked myself this question: if I were going to construct a course reading list of five books of *prose* that I hoped would spark interesting discussion among a group of graduate student poets, what might they be? With *this* as my working premise, I can offer–from among many contenders–the following:

1) *The Gutenberg Elegies* by Sven Birkerts, an intelligent, soulful mourning for the passing of the printed page and of the sensibilities and neurological patterns that respond to the printed page. 2) *The Gift* by Lewis Hyde, which begins in studying gift-giving in myth and fairy tale and anthropological studies, and ends in considering the implications of being "gifted" as a creative artist. 3) *On the Nature of the Universe* by Lucretius, the ancient Roman scientific-philosophical cosmology that shows how many nineteenth, twentieth, and now twenty-first century understandings of the world were predated by the rigorous thinking of Lucretius and his circle. [This pairs interestingly with Mary Shelley's *Frankenstein*, when it's considered for its chilling prescience.] 4) *In the Blink of An Eye* by Walter Murch, a book-length aesthetics of film editing by the head editor for a number of "literary films" like *Apocalypse Now* and *The Unbearable Lightness of Being*: both the bonds and the glitches between his work and the writer's make for fascinating reading. 5) *After the Revolution* by Joseph J. Ellis, the historian's study of the roots of

American literature and visual art in colonial times, looking both at individual practitioners and at the cultural assumptions that surrounded them. Beyond these five...I'll add that two recent books by Wendy Kaminer look interestingly at shaped thinking versus our climate's more prevalent tendency toward fuzzy thinking, and they context the reading of poetry in enabling ways.

Of course I've seen a (partial, but substantial) list of the poets contributing to this collection, and one could claim that they form an uber-list of reading possibilities...that there's little need to seek out the books these authorities *recommend* until one already knows and loves the books the authorities *created*.

GABRIEL GUDDING

Sir Thomas Browne, *Pseudodoxia Epidemica: An Enquiry into
    Common and Vulgar Errors*, ed. Robin Robbins
Willard Bascom, *Waves and Beaches: The Dynamics of the Ocean Surface*
Flann O'Brien, *At Swim-Two-Birds*
Robert Burton, *Anatomy of Melancholy*
Seneca, *Moral Essays*, trans. John Basore (volumes 1-3)
*No One May Ever Have the Same Knowledge Again: Letters to the
    Mount Wilson Observatory*, 1915-1935, edited and transcribed by
    Sarah Simons

The list of poetry books that have influenced me is so long and
the influence of each of the books in that list so complex and subtle that,
as I think over the possible candidates for such a list, each book seems
itself so imbricated and complicated in the various features and aspects of its
influences, that I cannot begin to list those books here in any meaningful
way without writing an essay on each of the most influential ones. In
addition, I suspect that my reasons for having been influenced by some
poetry books run counter to the "normal" reasons why certain books might
be considered influences. For instance, I have been influenced greatly by
font style and size in some books, by the visual layout favored by some
poets, etc etc. Because of this I will turn instead to those non-poetry
books that have altered profoundly my sense of the possibilities of poetry
and thought and, what, for want of a better phrase, could be called the life
of the imagination, each doing so in unique and unambiguous ways.
    Pseudodoxia Epidemica is an encyclopedia of commonly held
fallacies about the natural and anthropological worlds. Not only is the
book's content mad but Browne's syntax and prose rhythms are at times
and by turns so jarring and delightful, with Robbins keeping Browne's
original spelling, punctuation and capitalization, that the overall texture
of the writing, from content to appearance on the page, is profoundly
cacographical and stimulating.
    Willard Bascom's classic, *Waves and Beaches*, with utmost
patience and order, via a progression of what must be the clearest paragraphs
written by an oceanographer, describes the formal and formulaic aspects
of waves, berms, sand pit domes, rip channels and other features common
to waves and beaches. I came away from this book believing that a
Shaker had designed water. But it is the clarity with which complex and
seemingly chaotic phenomena are explained, diagrammed, and ordered
that gave me hope that it is possible to think about my own poetics and
to describe and teach something as complex as poetry. I have read this

book several times.

In Flann O'Brien's *At Swim-Two-Birds* the characters turn mutinous against the narrator and author. Need I say more?

What I have enjoyed about *Anatomy of Melancholy*, this large and undisciplined book, since I first read it in 1993, is its marriage of intellectual worlds, worlds that are now separated–namely the medical, psychological, historical, the philological and classical. The book helps me remember literature's true possibilities, which are to melt, meld, mix and make new understandings for the purpose of helping us live better, happier, and more fulfilling lives. The book's seeming indiscipline and encyclopedic comprehensiveness are at once an antidote to melancholy and a reminder of the palliative powers of writing. Too, I love (and I suppose this really is a simple-minded thing to love) but I love the way the book, a common feature of books of this time, interlards prose with poetry throughout. It reminds me that great art, like great medicine, is about mixing often disparate ingredients.

Seneca is someone I unfailingly return to when poetry fails me.

No One May Ever Have the Same Knowledge Again is a book of fascinating but totally mad and, I guess, "ignorant" letters written to the astronomers at the Mount Wilson Observatory by laypeople who earnestly want to convey their individual and often bizarre understandings about the stars, planets, geometry, cosmological origins, and other features of the universe. Theories contained in the letters are arrived at by the writers' own experiments or intuition. So captivating and happy-making are the letters, stuffed as they are with non-sequitur and invention, they'll reach anyone lost in the farthest grief (trust me, I know); they stand, for me, as testimonies to the glorious resourcefulness of the human imagination, of poesis, in the face of appalling ignorance and scant access to facts. I adore this book.

THOM GUNN

William Shakespeare
John Donne
Charles Baudelaire
William Carlos Williams
Basil Bunting, *Briggflatts and Other Poems*

   This list certainly says more about me than about the needs of any other poet. But you asked for it, and this is the truth. First, the obvious: I read all of Shakespeare in the summer vacation at the end of my first year at college, which I did mainly for my studies, but also for enjoyment. The way I did it, it came to about one play a day. I was also writing poetry, with more confidence than ever before. I was about 22 (we went to the university in England older than we would today). My poetry, for various reasons, benefited from this reading. (Another reason was that I was growing up, a little belatedly.)
   Second and third, John Donne's poetry and Baudelaire's poetry, both of whom I read in my late teens and early twenties, pretty constantly. I wanted to be John Donne in my twenties. I want to be Baudelaire now, the mature Baudelaire (I also want to be mature).
   Fourth, rather obviously, I was completely turned around by reading through all of William Carlos Williams. It is obvious that I learned how to write free verse from studying him.
   These have been the essentials for me. I also read everybody I could, and I don't know how to discriminate between them. From my friend Chaucer, to my friend August Kleinzahler, they have given me pause and helped me in my life and also in my writing. If I have to choose a fifth, I would say it is Basil Bunting's *Briggflatts*, which I came to late and advise for its huge inclusiveness and beauty. For me it is the greatest poem of the last century. Better than Pound, better than Eliot, better than Williams or Stevens.

SAM HAMILL

Kenneth Rexroth, *Complete Poems*
Walt Whitman, *Leaves of Grass*
Denise Levertov, *The Poetry of Denise Levertov*
Shunryu Suzuki, *Zen Mind, Beginner's Mind*
Jim Harrison, *The Shape of the Journey: Collected Poems*
Basho, *Oku no hosmomichi (Narrow Road to the Interior and
      Other Writings)*
Crossing the Yellow River: Three Hundred Poems from the Chinese,
      ed. Sam Hamill
Zen Flesh, Zen Bones, compiled by Paul Reps and Nyogen Senzaki
Hayden Carruth, *Collected Shorter Poems and Collected Longer Poems*
Czeslaw Milosz, *Collected Poems*

I believe that for poets what is most important is not so much individual books as a deep engagement with particular writers. That's how we begin to define our individual literary ancestry.

Rexroth's poems, translations, and essays shaped my commitment to poetry, as well as my very ethos.

Walt Whitman, the first truly "American" poet, advised us to "Resist much, obey little."

I list *The Poetry of Denise Levertov*, rather than one specific book, because I have read her poetry and essays for forty years. Her essays on "the line" are indispensable. And her poetry is a grand body of work that makes me proud to be a poet.

Suzuki-roshi's wonderful book is probably the best introduction to Zen in English, a book that I've been returning regularly to for many years. My practice is Zen. My practice is poetry. These are not two things.

Harrison's poetry is like no other.

I spent nearly ten years translating Basho. His Zen insights and poetry and prose are nonpareil.

The poetry of ancient China, which I collected in *Crossing the Yellow River*, taught me how to live. Simple as that. Tu Fu, Wang Wei, T'ao Ch'ien, and the others translated and collected here represent a quarter century of devoted study of Zen poetry and its traditions. They shaped my values and my imagination.

The Zen parables, koans, and poems in *Zen Flesh, Zen Bones* are essential. "Lightning flashes, / Sparks shower. / In one blink of your eyes / You have missed seeing."

Collected Shorter Poems and Collected Longer Poems of Hayden

Carruth is a two-volume "collected" that represents one of the most original and compelling poets of the last fifty years.

Missing from this list: The poems and essays of Adrienne Rich. Not in one particular book, but through her fierce commitment in poetry and essays, Rich's writing has had a profound effect on my life and writing. The same may be said of Ezra Pound, William Carlos Williams, Pablo Neruda, and W. S. Merwin.

JOY HARJO

James Welch, *Riding the Earthboy 40*
Pablo Neruda, *Captain's Verses*
Okot p'Bitek, *Song of Lawino*
Adrienne Rich, *Diving into the Wreck*
Audre Lorde, *The Black Unicorn*

Simon Ortiz urged me to read the fantastic poet and novelist, James Welch, from Montana, when I began writing in Albuquerque in the early seventies. *Riding the Earthboy 40*, his only book of poetry, was influential for many of us. It is still one of the classics of American Indian poetry.

I always smile when asked about Jim. In my catalogue of memories he's always leaning into that enigmatic grin, with some humorous comment, some angle of vision that made a grease so we could slide through the pain in this world a little easier. Beneath the eternal winters of human suffering and relentless cold, you could count on that sideways vision.

One of my favorite stories involving Jim was told to me by Simon, about the time he and Jim performed at a university in Buffalo, New York with a well-known Jewish writer who "translated" indigenous songs though he didn't know tribal languages. He sang and chanted his performance, even shook rattles and drummed. Jim and Simon read without fanfare in their pressed slacks and button down shirts. After the reading the Jewish man was inundated by attention from audience members who loved the performance of real Indian poetry, while Jim and Simon, the real Indians, stood virtually ignored to the side. We laughed about it. I can hear Jim telling the story, too, in a pub in upstate New York, with his finely tuned self-deprecatory style adding to the tale.

Jim left this world August 2003. I returned to his poetry, to the first full-length book of poetry by a native poet I had ever held in my hands. His poetry taught me that the human soul is utterly intertwined with the larger movements of land and history. And that there is a terrible humor born in tragedy, as in his poem "Harlem, Montana: Just off the Reservation."

Neruda's *Captain's Verses* was given to me by a friend and mentor, Geary Hobson, a Chickasaw professor and writer then teaching at the University of New Mexico. He looked out for me as I recklessly reeled through my young life. On one hand, I was a fool for desire and escape. On the other, I was responsible and studious. Neruda urged me to stop and listen passionately to the common sense of the mountains, to the hills and valleys within us. Being in love meant joining the earth and the sky, ecstatically, within us.

Neruda was esteemed by many young native poets. You can hear Neruda's influence in our early poetry. Maybe we thought of him as Indian, too, as he was a poet whose work was available to us, who spoke of the earth and the body with reverence. The Puritans had nearly destroyed that connection in the cultural overlay they provided as the template of the so-called "American Dream." Native cultures were to be usurped and destroyed. The soul was to deny the primitive instincts of the body. They had forgotten how to see the seamlessness of spirit. Neruda reminded me of the connection. And how what is simple is born of a terrible complexity. One of my favorite poems of his is "The Potter":

> Your whole body has
> a fullness or a gentleness destined for me.
>
> When I move my hand up
> I find in each place a dove
> that was seeking me, as
> if they had, love, made you of clay
> for my own potter's hands.
>
> Your knees, your breasts,
> your waist
> are missing parts of me like the hollow
> of a thirsty earth
> from which they broke off
> a form,
> and together
> we are complete like a single river,
> like a single grain of sand.

As a beginning poet I was ravenous for poetry that crooned and shouted and included the body in the spirit's journey for sense in this lower world. I devoured and was fed by the poetry of Leroi Jones/Amiri Baraka, June Jordan, Gwendolyn Brooks, Michael Harper, and other Black American poets. Historically, too, this connection made sense, as we were all descended from peoples who came up or through the South, via migrations from forced removals, from as far back as the 1600's. Also, we were all involved in making art from our redefined and newly entwined traditions. I don't know how I first knew of the classic long poem, *Song of Lawino*, by Okot p'Bitek. But I heard the struggle of the Mvskoke people in it, as we were forced from lands and traditions that held great meaning for us, into a false culture of commerce and Christianity. This poem is the fury song of a nation wronged by the forces of colonization, in the voice of a woman who is losing her husband to a woman of the new ways. P'Bitek translated the poem from his native Acoli tongue. I met him in Amsterdam in 1980 at the One World Poetry Festival. It was one of the highlights of my life.

I turn to Adrienne Rich for her burning intellect and her unwillingness to compromise on behalf of justice. In the poems of *Diving into the Wreck* she names the journey, and commits herself. Absolutely. These are poems that changed my life. And provoke the question I must always ask, Am I willing to sacrifice being comfortable for an integrity of vision? The title poem is a classic and marks a collective dive by the female powers in this ravaged land to bring up from the deep that which had been lost, denied, and misnamed.

The Black Unicorn first came to my attention through Audre's recitation of these poems in Minnesota at the Great Midwestern Bookfair in the early 1980's. I was struck by the sensual mythic tangle and power in these poems. I heard the voice of a warrior in the middle of a country born from Puritanism, wild hopes and violence. And was in awe of how these stunning flowers of poems had sprouted up from the steaming mess. When she read "Fog Report" that day from the stage I boldly (and uncharacteristically from the audience) asked her to read it again. And she did. The poem from this collection that most influenced me was the following poem, "A Litany for Survival." It inspired both "Anchorage" and "I Give You Back" from my book *She Had Some Horses*.

A Litany for Survival

For those of us who live at the shoreline
standing on the constant edges of decision
crucial and alone
for those of us who cannot indulge
the passing dreams of choice
who love in the doorways coming and going
in the hours between dawns
looking inward and outward
at once before and after
seeking a now that can breed
futures

like bread in our children's mouths
so their dreams will not reflect
the death of ours;

For those of us
who were imprinted with fear
like a faint line in the center of our foreheads
learning to be afraid with our mother's milk
for by this weapon
this illusion of some safety to be found
the heavy-footed hoped to silence us
For all of us
this instant and this triumph
We were never meant to survive.

And when the sun rises we are afraid
it might not remain
when the sun sets we are afraid
it might not rise in the morning
when our stomachs are full we are afraid
of indigestion
when our stomachs are empty we are afraid
we may never eat again
when we are loved we are afraid
love will vanish
when we are alone we are afraid
love will never return
and when we speak we are afraid
our words will not be heard
nor welcomed
but when we are silent
we are still afraid

So it is better to speak
remembering
we were never meant to survive.

MICHAEL S. HARPER

James Weldon Johnson, *God's Trombones: Seven Negro Sermons in Verse*
Jean Toomer, *Cane*
Melvin B. Tolson, *Harlem Gallery*
Melvin B. Tolson, *Libretto for the Republic of Liberia*
Sterling A. Brown, *Collected Poems*
Langston Hughes, *Collected Poems*
Robert Hayden, *Collected Poems*
Gwendolyn Brooks
Margaret Walker
Sherley Anne Williams
Rita Dove

God's Trombones: Seven Negro Sermons in Verse, "Go Down Death" in particular, is in that tradition which kept black people alive in their humanity, despite the affliction of white supremacy. (See Johnson's *American Negro Poetry* as a premier first anthology.)

Cane is an American classic in literary form: narrative, poetry and drama; a spellbinding tour de force in literary modernism and the folk.

Tolson's *Libretto for the Republic of Liberia* has a supercilious introduction, to be recorded and discounted.

Sterling A. Brown's *Collected Poems* is often mistaken as derivative, "vernacular" poetry, when it is pioneering authentic "folk" poetry, mostly dramatic portraits, written in a distinct folk idiom; pioneering because no actual person spoke like that, but providing the illusion that you are in the hands of a master wordsmith and raconteur. (See also Brown's *The Negro Caravan* with the best essay on folk literature, and a great deal more. For those interested in the craft, begin with a close scrutiny of "Vestiges" section and Brown's influences, Petrarch, Milton, Shakespeare, Wordsworth, Coleridge, Housman, and Hardy.)

Langston Hughes' *The Collected Poems*: many of these poems should be framed by Hughes' commitment to people in short stories, blues, newspaper columns, particularly through the views of Jesse B. Semple and Hughes' collaborations with Hurston and Bontemps.

Hayden was a 'romantic realist' who abandoned his nationalist poems written in the 1930's, though he was a master of literary conceits, including innovative ballads, the seminal "Middle Passage" (with special indebtedness to Rukeyser's "Amistad" chapter in her biography of Willard Gibbs), and "Black Spear" manuscript from Hopwood winning manuscript at University of Michigan, selected by W. H. Auden, his only mentor; a believer in peace when it was not fashionable, did not write on

Detroit riot of 1943 for example, and teacher of many students active in the civil rights movement of Nashville and Fisk University, where he was writer in residence, and a preparer of five-courses per semesters for over twenty-two years. Among his many classics: "The Diver," "The Rabbi," "Belsen, Day of Liberation," "Mourning Poem for the Queen of Sunday" (his burial portrait of the singer, Lula Butler Hurst), "Witch Doctor," and his experiments with the sonnet form: "Frederick Douglass," after Hopkins, "Those Winter Sundays," a poem for his stepfather, an exercise in the periodic sentence; and dramatic portraits: "El-Hajj Malik El-Shabazz" (Malcolm X), "Aunt Jemima of the Ocean Waves," and poems on the artistic process: "A Plague of Starlings," "The Night-Blooming Cereus," "Free Fantasia: Tiger Flowers," "Astronauts" and "American Journal." (See also *Collected Prose* for essential interviews and commentary on religion and history and American traductions of the truth in lore.)

Read everything by Gwendolyn Brooks. Brooks is master of the sonnet-ballad. Her "We Real Cool" is the best and shortest ballad of early death among black neighborhood males; in fact, she is mistress of her neighborhood, that area of Chicago she has documented and imagined as no sociologist can fathom, with or without theory. Her change of heart regarding America and *Blacks* should be noted in the classic transformation she experienced at Fisk University in 1966. Her service to all communities, her own and the world of letters, and caring, is legendary. Called "Mother Africa" by friend and foe alike, for her political stands, and for her bounty.

Read everything by Margaret Walker. *For My People* is an American classic; also her novel *Jubilee*, Vyrey is a seminal character in our literature. Also a master teacher and 'politician' "in a land most strange," Jackson, Mississippi.

Sherley Anne Williams: *The Peacock Poems*, *Some One Sweet Angel Chile*. Other: *Give Birth to Brightness* (criticism), *Dessa Rose* (novel), *Working Cotton* (fiction). Her "Letters from a New England Negro" takes a candid view of slavery as practiced mostly in the north, Providence Plantations and Rhode Island. "Give Birth to Brightness" was her MA thesis written at Brown University. She always credited her teachers, Sterling A. Brown and Philip Levine, as mentors. Seemed to extenuate her learning, the result of the cotton fields of San Joaquin valley rather than the library, where she spent many years mastering her idioms.

Read everything by Rita Dove. Playful and deadline serious in all her ventures at literary form, and a writer with perfect pitch, works diligently to embrace all aspects of her experience, geography, and interior landscape. Her interviews belie her efforts toward self-mastery in all the arts. A cosmopolitan who began in Akron but won't end there.

LOLA HASKINS

101 Favorite Poems, circa 1929, The Core Company
Yasunari Kawabata, *Palm of the Hand Stories*
William Butler Yeats, *The Collected Yeats*
Another Republic: 17 European & South American Writers, ed. Charles
    Simic
Henry James, *Barbarella and Other Stories*
Ranier Maria Rilke, *The Book of Images*, trans. Edward Snow
The Oxford Book of Verse
Amos Tutuola, *The Palm Wine Drinkard*

How I did this:

I loved the idea of this anthology, but it led me–I admit–into some serious avoidance. How COULD I choose just a few books out of a lifetime of reading? It seemed impossible. I knew that no matter what I did, I'd remember an even more essential something the minute it was too late to change my mind. Besides, who am I anyway? There must be lots of people whose choices would be more thoughtful than mine. Eventually, though, I got over the who-would-care misgiving, and convinced myself that I didn't really have to choose the ONLY possible books.

All that resolved, I had to decide what "essential" means to me as a poet, and, after some soul-searching, came to the conclusion that the *sine qua non* for me is inspiration. This moved reference books out of contention (they wouldn't be sufficient; therefore, they weren't essential) and brought non-poetry books in, because they've reminded me over and over of how poetry *feels* and what it can be.

With this preface, here are some books:

101 Favorite Poems: This little collection contains the poems I remember reading as a child, standards like "The Highwayman," "Sea Fever," "If," "For A' That and A' That," "The Bells," "Oh Captain, My Captain," and on and on, the most modern selection being "Mending Wall." There's an oval portrait of each poet with his or her poem. A lot of the poems are dated now, and many come off as sentimental, but that doesn't matter. I turn the pages and keep saying to myself oh yes, THAT one, I'd almost forgotten THAT one. And I'm back to that sense of magic that made me love poetry in the first place. I don't ever want to forget how that feels.

Palm of the Hand Stories: These are short shorts (written long before the current vogue for microfiction). I find Kawabata's work, especially the first scene in *Snow Country*, passionately compelling because of the economy and, therefore, resonance of its imagery. I picked *Palm of the*

Hand over *Snow Country*, though—first, for the wildness of some of its plots (unique as far as I know in Kawabata's work)—and second, because of one story, "The Grasshopper and the Bell Cricket," which to me is EXACTLY what poetry is about. It is, to put it simply, the most beautiful small story I have ever read.

   The Collected Yeats: No one writes sublimely all the time, and many of the poems in this book don't matter to me, but often over the years, when a friend quotes something that takes my breath away, it turns out to be Yeats. The eloquence of the Irish in general, and Yeats in particular, is something I'd like to keep inside.

   Another Republic: 17 European & South American Writers: The poets in this anthology have the varieties of hearts for words which send me into unexplored areas of my own excitements. Over many years, the transcendent minds in this book, and their own individual collections, have been super-valuable to me as sources of inspiration.

   Barbarella and Other Stories: James' labyrinths, both linguistic and psychological, absolutely thrill me. What I like best about them is how complicated they really are. My own work tends to the straightforward, and it's often too obvious, at least to me. As an antidote to that, I have James. He holds my head with both hands, and makes me look into dark funhouse-mirrors, where my emotions are starkly rendered in a way I wouldn't have come to without him.

   The Book of Images: Rilke sings the way no one else can. And I like this translation because it feels natural in English. As I imagine is obvious, I need a variety of voices. If I read only what sounds like me, I run the risk of self-imitation, something I've worked very hard to avoid. Whether I've succeeded or not, I don't know. I can only say that the sense of being in unknown territory is critical to me as a writer. When writing poetry slides to routine for me, and I can't find a way to break that, then I hope I'll have the grace to stop.

   The Oxford Book of English Verse: I feel as if I'm copping out, in a way, by picking this one, but it's such a case full of jewels, and though I think many, even most, of the 20th century inclusions won't stand the test of time, there are others like Louis MacNiece, Stevie Smith, and Philip Larkin, that I think will. And I like going back in time the way this book allows me to, and getting drunk on old favorites. Besides, every time I open it, I find some poem I hadn't known before, which puts me in that same high state. It's like you thought you knew your town. But then one day you take a turn you never took before, because it hadn't led to any of the places you usually go, and there it is, a little house almost concealed in the woods. And you can't forget it because, you realize, you always knew it was there.

The Palm Wine Drinkard: I'm including this book, a novel, because of the idiosyncrasy of its world view, both in language and plot. Tuotola opened something for me that's never quite closed, and I go back to him when I feel stale, to see how fresh words can really be.

I'm going to end my list here. Instead of ten, I'll include only these eight books, so I can leave places at the table for the most urgent two I will have forgotten. Alternatively, here are places for you, the reader, to add your own entries to my list, the ones that when you get to the end you're saying to yourself, how could she have left X out? And what about Y? *Whatever was she thinking?*

BOB HICOK

Chilton's Manual for a 1968 VW Beetle
Howard Zinn, *A People's History of the United States*
The Antaeus Anthology, ed. Daniel Halpren
Helen Gardner, *Art Through the Ages*
The Encyclopedia of Philosophy, ed. in chief, Paul Edwards

The Chilton manuals are guides to car repair. If you've owned a Bug–one of the originals–I don't need to tell you why this book was so important to me. If you've never owned a Bug, you're smarter than I am and can forego reading this list of books that have mattered to me. I can't remember how many times my red Bug with mag wheels and theoretical heat broke down on the highway, but like all good Chilton's, mine was grease stained and kicked more than once into a field.

I loved *A People's History of the United States* before *Good Will Hunting*. Along with Barbara Tuchman and David McCullough, Zinn writes history with a narrative flair. I also admire his admission that he writes from a particular perspective, that his aim is to speak for those less often heard: "Thus, in that inevitable taking of sides which comes from selection and emphasis in history, I prefer to tell the story of the discovery of America from the viewpoint of the Arawaks, of the Constitution from the standpoint of the slaves, of Andrew Jackson as seen by the Cherokees..." I first read this book in my early twenties, and his approach was radically refreshing.

Antaeus was one of my favorite literary publications, but I came to it late in its life and after reading this anthology. This is one of the first books of poetry I read. One of the oddest things about this book is that I like many of the poems by poets whose work I don't generally care for. I think Halpren got the best a poet had to offer. My copy is covered in a fair amount of duct tape–not duck tape, for those of you who read with colloquial eyes. I can't remember why *Antaeus* was closed down, but I say here that I'd like it back. Please.

I own two copies of Gardner's *Art Through the Ages*, for reasons of forgetfulness I think but also I couldn't pass up buying the second copy for $4.00. As the introduction states, "Since publication of the first edition in 1926, *Art Through the Ages* has been a favorite with generations of students and general readers, who have found it an exciting and informative survey." Poets are dilettantes, I am a poet, I am a dilettante. I'm also drawn to the arts, particularly painting, as many poets–slaves to the image–are. Whereas most textbooks have the effect on the mind that English cooking has on the stomach, Gardner moves with spry thoroughness through the development of Western art. And the book does not stint on images.

Paul Edwards is the Editor in Chief of *The Encyclopedia of Philosophy*. Editor in Chief is a more satisfying title, don't you think? Certainly such a person would get the best parking space. I enjoy this affair in four volumes, covering Abbagnano through Zubiri, because the mind-body problem is something few people want to talk about. I like reference books, and this is my favorite example of the species. Can't remember what bee was in Hume's bonnet, who the heroes of deontological ethics were? This is the book for you. As Americans, we are enthralled by action and afraid of deliberation. Poets feel they're overlooked: name a contemporary philosopher. Self-reflection may be the highest art; I like to be reminded we are capable of at least trying to take ourselves apart.

TONY HOAGLAND

Wallace Stevens, *Harmonium*
Charles Simic, *Return to a Place Lit by a Glass of Milk*
James Tate, *The Lost Pilot*
Frank O'Hara, *Selected Poems*
Jon Anderson, *In Sepia*
Robert Pinsky, *The Situation of Poetry*
Larry Levis, *Winter Stars*
Jack Myers, *As Long as You're Happy*
John Skoyles, *A Little Faith*
John Engman, *Keeping Still, Mountain*

My first great desire in poetry was to be a poet of ideas. When I lived in Ithaca, New York, in the late seventies, working as a night time janitor at Cornell University Press, reading my way through the Ithaca Public Library's excellent poetry section, I remember coming across some reissued memorial edition of Stevens' *Harmonium*. Knowing so little, I still was struck by the lightness of Stevens; I hated Stevens' cannonical touchstone poems–"Ideas of Order at Key West," and "Sunday Morning" were Greek to me–but I understood the whimsical lyrics about language and perception, and I heard the music. (In that same era I found A. R. Ammons' very cool early books, vanity press productions, and also idea-driven.)

But I didn't have the music or probably the intellectual strength to be a poet of ideas. Simic's early Antheneum books, *Dismantling the Silence* and *Return to a Place Lit by a Glass of Milk*, were a tutorial in the clean radiance of image. That was the sole skill I was able to cultivate in my early writing. A teacher had aimed me at James Tate's surrealist books (*The Oblivion Ha-Ha*), which ruined my writing for at least two years, two years of intoxication with word combinations and verbal hallucinations. But I recovered, eventually, and *The Lost Pilot* showed me how narrative and wordplay could supplement each other. Reading Robert Pinsky's critical book, *The Situation of Poetry*, taught me an enormous amount, especially about diction in his discussion of Berryman and Ransom. That book is still a treasurehouse of poetical intelligence.

Other books: *In Sepia*, by Jon Anderson was a crucial inspiration for many poets of my generation. Poems like "Refusal," "John Clare," and "In Autumn" united thinking, serious meditation, lyricism, and a deliciously elegiac sensibility. This book, which seems to be entering forgetfulness, shaped poets like Levis, David Wojahn, and others.

Other books which had a big impact on me were *A Little Faith* by John Skoyles, with its intelligence, wry humanity, and clarity of style; *As Long as You're Happy*, by Jack Myers, a comic and muscular book full of duende, was very influential to me; and *Keeping Still, Mountain* by John Engman, who died young, and whose press, Gallileo, also went under after some truly great books. *The Incognito Lounge*, of course, blew everyone up; Norman Dubie was endemically contagious. I was yet to find and understand O'Hara and Merwin. But these are some of the most important books to me as a young poet.

PAUL HOOVER

César Vallejo, *Trilce*, trans. David Smith
Thomas Traherne, "Shadows in the Water"
Lorine Niedecker, *Collected Works*
Stevie Smith, *Selected Poems*
Wallace Stevens, *The Collected Poems*
Fernando Pessoa, *Selected Poems*
Charles Simic, *Selected Poems*
John Ashbery, *The Tennis Court Oath*
Amiri Baraka, "The Rare Birds"

INNOCENCE AND CALCULATION

This list helps me to realize the range of my own leanings and, more importantly, where my true affections lie. I love the New York School of poets– Ashbery, O'Hara, Schuyler, Koch, and Guest–but finally it's the variety offered by the whole that inspires me as a reader. If I had to choose from the heart, it would be "Korean Mums" by James Schuyler. I love Schuyler's knowing innocence, his fully open eyes. This is also what impresses me about Vallejo, Traherne, and Niedecker (I might have added John Clare): the sweetness and acceptance with which they view the world. Stevie Smith's mind is colder, her ironies fiercer. Innocence wants to open, reveal, and believe. Its natural mode is the lyrical. But poetry also wants some degree of calculation. That's where irony, complication, and strategy come in. Among the many who also might have been named are George Herbert, Carlos Drummond de Andrade, Hart Crane, Emily Dickinson, Jaime Sabines, and a variety of contemporary Americans including Caroline Knox, Ann Lauterbach, Michael Palmer, and Fanny Howe.

Without *Trilce*, I couldn't conceive of writing poetry. Like all good poetry, it combines familiarity and strangeness. In their attempt to grasp the absolute, the surrealists embraced strangeness too strongly. It left no room for familiar things, like peeling a banana or standing outside your dead parent's door. One part of *Trilce* contains the familiar: "Tonight I climb down from the horse / at the front door of my house, where / I said goodbye with the rooster crowing. / It's locked and no one answers." Another part offers the madness of language that poetry uniquely offers: "Distill this 2 in a single shift / and between the two of us we'll speed it up. / Nobody heard me. Hot fluting / civil abracadabra."

Traherne's poem, "Shadows in the Water," can be found in

Seventeenth Century Poetry: The Schools of Donne and Jonson, edited by Hugh Kenner. Kenner describes Traherne as "a shoemaker's son, a country clergyman" and "a gentle fanatic on such matters as simplified spelling and the ecstatic life." He writes a poetry of lavish beauty based on simple but magical observations, such as seeing himself reflected in a body of water: "Thus did I walk by the Water's brink / Another World beneath me think; / And while the lofty spacious Skies / Reverse'd there abus'd mine Eyes, / I fancy'd other Feet / Came mine to touch and meet / As by some Puddle I did play / Another World within it lay." Though he lived briefly from 1637 to 1674, Traherne's manuscripts were not discovered until 1903. I love the innocence and calculation of his eye, an innocence that lies on the side of indeterminacy.

Lorine Niedecker, *Collected Works*: Here is a poetry of emotional size despite the smallness and innocence of it's world: "You are my friend / you bring me peaches / and the high bush cranberry / you carry / my fishpole / you water my worms / you patch my boot / with your mending kit / nothing in it / but my hand." Niedecker's work has the precision, discretion, and materiality of an Objectivist but allows for personal observation. Such poetry reveals the rhetorical excesses and indiscretion of the confessional approach. "Life's dance: / they meet / he holds her leg / up." There's an innovative American poetry that passes from modernist women like Niedecker and Moore to Fanny Howe and Elizabeth Robinson without encountering much of Gertrude Stein. Its means of seeing includes the metaphysical. In Howe's collection *Veteran*: "Some of the others believe in food & drink & perfume / I don't. And I don't believe in shut-in time / for those who committed a crime / of passion. / Like a sweetheart / of the iceberg or wings lost at sea / the wind is what I believe in, / the One that moves around each form." Niedecker is reticent about the One, preferring the lower case singular. All share in the mystery of things as they are.

Stevie Smith sees the world complexly rather than sentimentally; that is, she sees the truth. Because it's married to fate, truth's humor is dark. "Harold's Leap," for instance: "Harold, I remember your leap, / it may have killed you. / But it was a brave thing to do." Smith's work asserts the kindness of death, for which, sadly, it receives little credit. Here is irony at its sweetest and most trenchant; it forgives as it condemns. Her best work includes "Mother, among the Dustbins," "Not Waving but Drowning," "To Carry the Child," and most especially the masterpiece "Pretty." Here's the ending of "God the Eater": "When I am dead I hope that he will eat / Everything I have been and not been / And crunch and feed upon it and grow fat / Eating my life all up as it is his." A resolute loneliness pervades the work, and this makes her loveable.

Stevens' work is lyrical and philosophical. It is therefore amusing, a play of mind amid the "pretty contrast of life and death." My first experience of Stevens, "Connoisseur of Chaos," with its balances, color, and wide-ranging depth, is among my most lasting. There are two major moods in his work: the wintry and the florid. I tend to prefer the wintry, as seen in "The Snow Man." My own poetry runs in the balance between Stevens and Williams, especially WCW's "The Botticellian Trees," which is to say between the plain and ornate, the direct and the oblique.

Of Pessoa's four personae as a poet, which included that of Pessoa himself, I prefer Alvaro de Campos, the "naval engineer and Sensationist poet." According to editor and translator Richard Zenith, "Various manifestos, including the Futurist Ultimatum of 1917, were signed by the naval engineer, who also got involved in Pessoa's private life, sometimes even writing letters to Pessoa's friends. It was Alvaro de Campos who proclaimed, "The best way to travel is to feel." One of his poems about travel ends: "The ports with their unmoving ships, / Intensely unmoving ships, / And small boats close by, waiting." Pessoa's work is beautifully quoted in the Wim Wenders film *Lisbon Story*. His project in mosaic identity reminds us how many poets we are in the course of a lifetime, as each poem demands a new identity.

Simic's poetry is mythic and therefore always a bit fictive, philosophical and therefore ironic. His poem "Bedtime Story" has all these qualities: "When a tree falls in a forest / And there's no one around / To hear the sound, the poor owls / Have to do all the thinking." At a time when the non-narrative increasingly has the ideological upper hand, it's useful to remember how many wonderful fictive poems (Robert Hayden's "Those Winter Sundays" or Gwendolyn Brooks' "The Mother") transcend self-consciousness and anecdotalism. Simic does so by locating figures so wry and essential that they seem to be remembered from dreams.

Ashbery is probably tired of hearing the importance of this early volume, *The Tennis Court Oath*. Nevertheless, this is one of the essential books of our period. Written by a young poet who thought his first collection, *Some Trees*, had come to nothing critically, it's reckless in its plunge and therefore completely invigorating. Every young poet should read this book for its range, tonal shifts, and freedom of reference, which redefined the lyric poem. For all its supposed wildness and "ridiculous / Vases of porphyry," the collection is filled with "beautiful dreams" and "grim engines."

"The Rare Birds" appeared in Baraka's 1987 volume *The Music* and later in the wonderful anthology *Moment's Notice: Jazz in Poetry &*

Prose, edited by Art Lange and Nathaniel Mackey. Here's the final stanza: "Williams writes to us / of the smallness of this American century, that it splinters into worlds it / cannot live in. And having given birth to the mystery / splits unfolds like gold shattered in daylight's beautiful hurricane / (praying Sambos blown apart) out of which a rainbow of anything you need. / I heard these guys. These lovely ladies, on the road to Timbuctoo / waiting for Tu Fu to register on the Richter scale. It was called / *Impressions*, and it was a message, from like a very rare bird." Highly recommended from the same anthology: "Giuffre's Nightmusic" by Thomas McGrath.

Baraka writes about giving birth to the mystery, McGrath about "dream-singing emblems" and a "ladder of slow bells." What I want from poems is something similar: a ceremony involving doubt, belief, magic, and a pleasant feeling of consternation.

FANNY HOWE

Years ago Edward Dahlberg gave me a list of ten books that I was allowed to read, all the rest being trash. Some of the trash included Melville, the Brontës, Thomas Hardy, Dickinson, Yeats, Rilke and Joyce. These writers have populated my bookshelves for decades. Dahlberg would have been repelled by anthologies that I own: Jerome Rothenberg's *America: A Prophecy*, *The Negro Caravan*, edited by Sterling Brown, Donald Allen's *New American Poetry*, *Moving Borders*, edited by Mary Margaret Sloan, and *Early Celtic Poetry*. He despised almost all fiction, and my large collection of contemporary fiction, which includes many friends and world poets, he would have called "an utter waste of time." I will not provide his approved list here. But I will say that Dahlberg's own autobiography, *Because I Was Flesh*, stays with me as an object and a model of enlightened prose literature. What would he make of that?

ANDREW HUDGINS

Homer
Euripides
Dante
William Shakespeare
Christopher Marlowe
Walt Whitman
Emily Dickinson
Rainer Marie Rilke
T. S. Eliot
William Butler Yeats
Robert Frost
King James Bible

Young writers have already read books that have thrilled them and changed them so profoundly that they now want to write. That's a given. To recommend to them the books that have thrilled and changed me is, then, an arrogant violation of their developing passions that I'm happy to indulge in.

What is easier than recommending the obvious? I'm happy to tell anyone to reread Homer, Euripides, Dante, Shakespeare, Marlowe, Whitman, Dickinson, Rilke, Eliot, Yeats, Frost, and the glorious *King James Bible*, though I haven't read all of them myself lately. Everyone agrees—my high voice singing at the edge of a vast chorus—that they are wonderful writers and crucial works, works great by any definition of greatness. And that list leaves out Keats and Chaucer, who cannot be left out. And Milton, and God knows who else. These writers see so deeply into what we, as humans, are, and write about it with such power and undiminished vitality that we experience their greatness over and over with each reading.

But sometimes their very greatness is overwhelming, their achievement so intimidating that it reduces beginning writers to awed and sullen silence, galled by their own shortcomings. It did me. That awareness, surprisingly enough, freed me to return to them with love and not resentment. By trying to be them and failing, I learned who I was. Or that's what I hope has happened. As an earthling, it is strange to labor, harvest, thresh, and die on a planet with dozens of suns and even more moons circling it, hundreds of asteroids blazing by on irregular orbits, and multi-colored stars stippling the night sky. I'll never forget the moment that I skipped ahead in my tenth grade English textbook and discovered Eliot's "The Hollow Men." I shivered with excitement. The poem, as much through its rhythm as its words, exactly captured a sense of the world that I did not know I had. It both confirmed what I thought and felt, and took me beyond thought and feeling to a deeper awareness of my consciousness. I understood that my self-consciousness was both a modern condition and essentially sentimental. The poem did all this with a powerful and insinuating rhythm that moved me beyond language via language.

Younger writers should have that hair-raising revelatory moment, or one like it. But who knows whose spirit will join with theirs and whether it will be a marriage or a fling? Something they will live their lives proud of or embarrassed by? And does it matter? They should also read and love writers who are wonderful and often dazzling, but less than great, as Auden did Hardy and as I did Auden—as well as Vaughn, Browne, Housmen, Millay, Plath, Lowell, and Dylan Thomas. But I also loved filthy limericks that I'm proud to shout hello to when I meet them on the street. It's when I meet my first great literary love, the man whose poems I committed to memory—that I blush and rush by. I barely mumble a greeting to Mr. Poe, as the unnerving and insistent sound of bells, probably funeral bells, repeats from blocks away.

LISA JARNOT

Allen Ginsberg, *Collected Poems*
Arthur Rimbaud, *Illuminations*
Jack Spicer, *The Holy Grail*
Robert Duncan, *Ground Work I: Before the War*
Bernadette Mayer, *The Bernadette Mayer Reader*
Frank O'Hara, *Selected Poems*
James Joyce, *Ulysses*

Allen Ginsberg and Lawrence Ferlinghetti were my first influences as a poet. (Bob Dylan had come earlier and it was through Dylan that I became aware of the Beat writers.) I love tradition. I've never been very exotic in my reading habits. I guess I'm a Beatnik at heart. Allen's writing literally saved my life. I read his poetry when I was a freshman in college. I was lonely and suicidal. He had been lonely and suicidal thirty years earlier. "A Supermarket in California" and "America" were the keys for me. I was a big misfit. I wanted to tell someone how I felt. Allen's poetry granted me that permission. The image of him "self-conscious with a headache" walking down a side street in Berkeley longing for Walt Whitman–that inspired me to be a poet.

The work of Rimbaud, and then Jack Spicer and Robert Duncan followed. A line from Rimbaud stays with me "I embrace the summer dawn." The immediacy of the energy of Rimbaud's poetry was a delight. Everything felt fresh and new and to the point. His teenaged angst must have also been appealing. And of course his idea that "I is another." It resonated with my intrigue regarding Bob Dylan's persona. I wanted to invent myself as a poet. Jack Spicer furthered that cause with his dry sense of humor and his incredible dedication to poetry. Spicer's *The Holy Grail* led me to Malory's work and Jessie Weston's *From Ritual to Romance*. In retrospect, Spicer seems to speak from the position of someone struggling with a Borderline Personality Disorder. His desire to relate to objects and his inability to do so is heartbreaking, but he managed to harness that pathology into his poetry in a clear fascinating way.

Robert Duncan's work didn't make sense to me when I started reading it. I thought maybe it was classic "nature poetry." While I was a student at the University of New York at Buffalo, I studied with Robert Creeley. In the classroom one day he read to us from Duncan's "The Venice Poem." He didn't have much to say about it except for that it was beautiful. I thought it was beautiful and complex and I wanted to know more about it. I was working at the Poetry/Rare Books Collection at the university and we had recently acquired Duncan's papers. I spent two and a half years reading all of Duncan's notebooks and becoming an amateur Duncan scholar of sorts. Duncan's dedication to being a craftsman of language has meant the world to me. His work held secrets that I was eager to unravel. His later work, particularly in *Ground Work I: Before the War* is still a source of unlimited pleasure and new rewards for me. The opening two poems stand as a tribute to H. D. and Pound, and the final poem "Circulations of the Song" is, I think, one of the great love poems of the English language. Duncan is an underappreciated master–I hope that he comes to hold a place near Shakespeare and Dante.

When I moved to New York City in 1994, it was partly because I was in love with the work of Bernadette Mayer and Frank O'Hara. Bernadette had visited Brown University while I was there as a graduate student in the MFA program. Her sense of play and of the possibilities of language was exhilarating. She loved the dictionary and she loved to learn about a variety of fields of knowledge. Her poetry became a cataloging place of everything that she had learned from the world. I was hooked. I can't name a single book of Bernadette's as an influence because I love them all. Her range is incredible, from sonnets to letters to book length projects to journals to dream writing and so on. Whenever I have a doubt about what to do next, I look to Bernadette for guidance. Frank O'Hara offered another kind of guidance–convincing me that poets take poetry too seriously. Through reading O'Hara I became interested in his European influences, especially Vladimir Mayakovsky. O'Hara is the one poet I can't figure out how to mimic. His poems seem simple, but they have a subterranean complexity to them. The ode form has always been appealing to me, and O'Hara's work is packed with odes. He sets the stage for all kinds of excitement with those killer lines–"You are gorgeous and I am coming" or "Don't be afraid of hatred, it lets love breathe."

James Joyce's *Ulysses* is a text I've relied on to have a better sense of the possibility of the parameters of a creative work. I love complex hidden orders and I'm obsessive about details. When I was a kid I loved to imagine whole worlds of my own making, away from the reality I lived in, but informed by it. Joyce's *Ulysses* is a space like that for me– complex and inviting and always seeming to change and expand. I like the arrogance of Joyce. I like it that he decided to make his own worlds in *Ulysses* and *Finnegan's Wake*, and I especially like it that he decided to make worlds based on his knowledge of history and literature. There are lines in Joyce that never leave my head. "The ineluctable modality of the visible." It doesn't matter what it means–it's a poem to me.

PETER JOHNSON

Kim Addonizio, *Tell Me*
The Poetry of Catullus, trans. G. H. Sisson
Stephen Dobyns, *Cemetery Nights*
Russell Edson, *The Reason Why the Closet Man Is Never Sad*
Max Jacob, *The Dice Cup: Selected Prose Poems*, ed. Michael Brownstein
Vladimir Nabokov, *Lolita*
Nicanor Parra, *Antipoems: New and Selected*, ed. David Unger
Charles Simic, *The World Doesn't End*
Bruce Smith, *The Other Lover*
James Tate, *Selected Poems*

MY FAVORITE BOOKS (AT LEAST FOR THIS WEEK)

Poets always complain about how difficult it is to publish books of poetry, yet hundreds appear every year, and many major poets seem to publish a new book every other year. Why? Partly because publishers will print anything they write; partly because they have jobs with little or no teaching, which frees up a tremendous amount of time. I mean, if you're getting paid a lot of money to teach one or two days a week, you better be writing something. The literary scene is indeed manic, as if whoever publishes the most poems is the best poet. Consequently, most books are thin at best, and if you leaf through the last three books of your favorite poet–books probably published within a four or five year period–you'll realize that if your favorite poet had been patient and chosen the best poems from his last three books, he would have written one of those volumes poets call their "favorite" books–ones they return to over and over again for solace, for inspiration, even for entertainment. Many of my favorite books, ones that continue to influence my own poetry and fiction, are classics such as Ovid's *Amores*, anything by Sappho or Shakespeare, Andreas Capellanus' *The Art of Courtly Love*, Voltaire's *Candide*, *Don Quixote*, *Gulliver's Travels*, and Novalis' and Kafka's short prose. But in compiling this list, except for one classical author, I decided to privilege some contemporary books I often reread whenever I'm bored or unable to write. Although I can think of at least ten more books, I'll stick with these for now–in alphabetical order:

Tell Me: No fluff here. Poem after poem rocks with cruelty and compassion. It's very easy to become self-indulgent or oversentimental when dealing with her subject matter. So easy to romanticize and idealize drunks and drug addicts, or to feel sorry for oneself or one's personal history or past mistakes. Yet, with dark irony, Addonizio embraces her own and everyone else's bumps and bruises. "I am going to stop thinking about my losses now," the narrator of the title poem says, "and listen to yours. I'm so sick of dragging them / with me wherever I go, like children up too late / who should be curled in their own beds."

The Poetry of Catullus: Whatever happened to invective–the fine art of skewering someone? Every night we're assaulted by the unreality of Reality TV, and every morning we're greeted by another stupid war, while our poets unashamedly hawk their poems like insurance salesmen or traveling medicine men. It's certainly time for another Catullus. "Thallus, you pansy, softer than rabbit's wool / The down of a goose or the lobe of an ear, / Softer than an old man's penis and the cobwebs hanging from it /...Give me back my cloak, you stole it..." Enough said.

Cemetery Nights: Probably my favorite contemporary book of verse poetry. A making of new myths and a wacky retelling of old ones, played out in a world overseen by a God wearing blinders. Yet amidst the absurdity and horror, optimism and compassion lurk. Consider this from the opening of "Cemetery Nights": "sweet dreams, sweet memories, sweet taste of earth: / here's how the dead pretend they're still alive, / one drags up a chair, a lamp, unwraps / the newspaper from somebody's garbage, / then sits holding the paper up to his face. / No matter if the lamp is busted and his eyes / have fallen out..." A contemporary classic.

The Reason Why the Closet Man Is Never Sad: When I first began writing and submitting prose poems, rejection slips came back, suggesting my poems were cheap imitations of Russell Edson's. Considering I had never heard of Edson, I was a bit shocked, yet believing you should at least read the authors you're influenced by, I bought *The Reason Why the Closet Man Is Never Sad*. I admire all of Edson's work–its apparent and seductive simplicity, its logical zaniness, its comic-book texture–but this particular book is his best. It's comic, for sure, but also characterized by what he calls the "dark uncomfortable metaphor," suggested by the "closet man" himself, who tries, hopelessly, of course, to control his life.

The Dice Cup: Selected Prose Poems: Edited and with an Introduction by Michael Brownstein, this is a book I never tire of. Constantly inventive and surprising, Jacob would have made a great stand-up comedian. He does with words what the Cubists did with paint, his greatest virtue being that he never took himself too seriously.

Lolita: How does one make us want to listen to a pedophile, or even like him? Unreliable narrators are scattered throughout my prose poetry and fiction, and Nabokov's book taught me how to keep them from becoming caricatures. Humbert Humbert sings, and we are seduced by his language while simultaneously questioning his erotic outbursts and lack of self-knowledge. "Lolita, light of my life, fire of my loins. My sin, my soul. Lo-lee-ta: the tip of the tongue taking a trip of three steps down the palate to tap, at three, on the teeth. Lo. Lee. Ta." Whoof!

Antipoems: New and Selected: "Maximum content, minimum words," Parra said. "Economy of language, no metaphors, no literary figures." Funny, angry, self-deprecating, politically savvy, skeptical of grand narratives, all the necessary talents to be a poet in our absurd times. Who else, after years of taunting us, would apologize for his poetry, ask us to burn his book, then say, "I take back everything I said"?

The World Doesn't End: This book of prose poems received a Pulitzer Prize in 1990, much to the dismay of many formalist poets, who were outraged that a book of prose poems could win such a prestigious award. I think it's Simic's best book, and I wish he would write more prose poems. The genre has always welcomed comic juxtapositions and the merging of different genres, making it a fertile place for Simic's prodigious imagination. The simplicity of this book still astounds me.

The Other Lover: A book that was up for a National Book Award the same year as Addonizio's *Tell Me*. All of Smith's talents come together here. Equally adept at formal patterns or the prose poem, he's a troubadour of lost love, a social critic, a blues-and-jazz man, both learned and hip. A very American book, with poems full of loss and love, all held together by wisdom and compassion.

Tate's *Selected Poems*: Constantly surprising, Tate is a comic genius. Marjorie Perloff argued that Rimbaud's "multiplicity of meaning gives way to a strange new literalism." Ditto for Tate. Reading his poems, I often feel as if I'm visiting another planet, governed by a philosopher king wielding a poo-poo cushion instead of Ex Caliber. Tate should be given an honorary Nobel Prize for his titles alone: "Same Tits," "Goodtime Jesus," "Teaching the Ape to Write Poems."

X. J. KENNEDY

Mother Goose
Robert Louis Stevenson, *A Child's Garden of Verses*
Walt Whitman, *Leaves of Grass*
The Rubaiyat of Omar Khayyam, trans. Edward Fitzgerald
Ralph Waldo Emerson, *Essays*
William Butler Yeats, *Collected Poems*
The English and Scottish Popular Ballads, ed. Francis J. Child
William Blake, *Songs of Innocence and Songs of Experience*

The books that make dents on one early in life are doubtless those that stay essential. Mother Goose and *A Child's Garden* were what I heard when, in my mother's lap, I attended my first poetry reading. The Mother Goose rhymes are metrically powerful: like bursts of bullets. They had to be tough to survive little changed through the centuries. Like Mother Goose, Stevenson's *Garden* is lilting, metrically amazing, and occasionally mysterious (see "The moon has a face like the clock on the wall..."). It's just as well that modern editions omit its smug Victorian colonial put-down of children whose diet is different from an English child's.

I grew up in the depressed 1930's when books were a luxury; but luckily, our family had a pile of Haldeman-Julius Little Blue Books—early paperbacks rattily printed on cheap paper and sold for a nickel apiece. There I discovered two books of verse that came from opposite poles: Walt Whitman beating his breast and shouting great psalm-like orations to the Long Island waves, and Edward Fitzgerald gorgeously mistranslating from the Persian old Omar's counsels to drink and screw because that's all there is. Whitman the clear-eyed affirmer of everything, Omar the atheistic cynic and tipsy sourpuss. Whitman with his open long-sustained lines, Omar with his tinkling jewel-like quatrains. I loved 'em both.

Another Little Blue Book contained Emerson's essay "Self-Reliance." Emerson, as is well known, isn't much of an original thinker; rather, he scrapes together other people's thoughts, chiseling them into epigrams. "Trust thyself: every heart vibrates to that iron string." I didn't know what an iron string was, and don't know to this day, but I liked that sentiment. I needed somebody to encourage me to trust my own quirky notions and do my idiosyncratic things. "Do your work," Ralph says, "and you shall reinforce yourself." And the same message informs his essay "The American Scholar": "Meek young men grow up in libraries, believing it their duty to accept the views which Cicero, which Locke, which Bacon have given; forgetful that Cicero, Locke, and Bacon were only young men in libraries when they wrote these books."

Yeats was a revelation. I met his work only in college, then spent four years in the Navy with his *Collected Poems* in my sea bag on every ship, in my locker at every shore station. I tried to imitate him, and wrote wretchedly. I discovered that Yeats can teach you a great deal about where to let the stress fall on a word, but that he can't be successfully imitated.

The best of the Child ballads and the Blake songs remain my touchstones for poetry. How many poems do you know any deeper and more powerful than "Sir Patrick Spens" or "The Unquiet Grave," better than "The Tyger," "The Sick Rose," or "London" ("I wander through each chartered street")? Those poems illustrate a truth that Ezra Pound insisted on in his wonderful *ABC of Reading* – by the way, another essential book – in poetry, only emotion endures.

DAVID KIRBY

William Blake, *The Marriage of Heaven and Hell*
Walt Whitman, *Leaves of Grass*
Allen Ginsberg, *Howl and Other Poems*
Dante, *The Inferno*, trans. Ciaran Carson (though John Ciardi's is just as
    good)
William Shakespeare, *Complete Works* (especially *Macbeth* and *Twelfth Night*)
John Keats, *Odes*
Little Richard, *The Essential Little Richard*
Barbara Hamby, *Babel*
Herman Melville, *Moby Dick*
Primo Levi, *If This Is a Man* and *The Truce* (in one volume; also
    published as *Survival in Auschwitz* and *The Reawakening*)

Last year, the city laid a sidewalk that intersected my driveway.
I've always felt there's something wrong with a person, even a grownup,
who doesn't want to write in wet concrete, but I must have telegraphed
my desires—too many how-you-guys-doing visits, too many furtive
glances out the den window—because the workers delayed the pouring.

Then one night we came home from a party, and sure enough, the
bastards had poured, even though there'd been only an empty frame in
the ground when we'd left. In fact, I'm sure they waited until we backed
out of the driveway and then dragged their equipment out of the bushes,
because the concrete was almost dry. Still, while my wife Barbara held
a flashlight, I went to work. I ruined a perfectly good TruValue screwdriv-
er and had to hold the light in my teeth after Barbara got tired and went
in, but in 45 minutes or so, I managed to scratch JOHN KEATS in one
corner where sidewalk and driveway intersected, LITTLE RICHARD
opposite it, and then, in the two corners that remained, WALT WHIT-
MAN and JANE AUSTEN (though I have to confess that I was thinking
as much of the bosomy film version of *Pride and Prejudice* as I was the author).

When people ask me what my favorite book is, which they do
frequently, I tell them this story. There are two points I'm trying to
make: one is that no writer loves just one book above all others; only
Playboy bunnies claim to read *Antigone* over and over. The second
point is that the list has got to be a little odd, both in terms of strange
bedfellows (Whitman and Austen) and the unexpected (Little Richard).
Just as original thinkers tend to be a little off kilter, so a good reading list is
asymmetrical; otherwise, you might as well just photocopy the table of
contents of the *Norton Anthology*.

After I tell that story, sometimes my questioner will say, "So those are your favorite artists, huh?" I tell them that I'm not trying to say "These are my favorite artists" but "This is the way a writer's mind works." And if someone ever asks me if I like Little Richard better than I like Keats, I'll answer with Montaigne's observation that raisins are the best part of a cake, though raisins aren't as good as a cake.

In compiling my list of 10 essential works, I begin with the three great dithyrambic poets of Western literature, Blake, Whitman, and Ginsberg, because that's my tradition. Next, I list Dante and Shakespeare, because I try to incorporate their majesty and rough humor. Keats is there because I want to borrow as much lushness from him as I can.

Little Richard is next on my list because I need him for rhythm. Here's an excerpt from a 1926 letter from Virginia Woolf to Vita Sackville-West; apparently Sackville-West had said that the right word makes or breaks a piece of writing, and Woolf replies: "As for the *mot juste*, you are quite wrong. Style is a very simple matter; it is all rhythm. Once you get that, you can't use the wrong words. But on the other hand here I am sitting after half the morning, crammed with ideas, and visions, and so on, and can't dislodge them, for lack of the right rhythm..." All the heavy furniture I get from Ginsberg and Dante and Shakespeare and Keats will get up and fly around the room if I can just get the right rhythm going. I also like Little Richard's speed, and, even though we're in different branches of show biz, his crowd appeal.

Having lit so many candles at the feet of what Keats calls "the mighty dead," I have to say that the poet I read the most is my wife, Barbara Hamby, author of *Delirium* and *The Alphabet of Desire* as well as *Babel*, which is forthcoming as I write but will be in print by the time this essay appears. Just as Barbara reads everything I write, so I read everything of hers. I've never known anyone to spend as much time as she does on a poem. Nothing leaves her desk until every word, every mark of punctuation, every margin and space has been weighed in the balance as if it were platinum. Barbara's writing practices bring mine up to a higher level, though I can't imagine anyone being as meticulous as she is.

So if I had to pack light for a desert island, these eight choices would be the ones I'd make. But if I had a little more room in my knapsack, I'd take the works by Melville and Primo Levi. These, too, hit the same notes of grandeur and joy that Dante and Shakespeare do; to a supple mind, laughter can be heard even in a death camp.

Now I'll have no respect at all for you, reader, if you merely copy my list and begin to read it. But I'll love you forever if you come up with a lopsided list of your own.

MAXINE KUMIN

Virgil, *The Aeneid*
Walt Whitman, *Selected Poems*, ed. Harold Bloom
Karl Shapiro, *Selected Poems*, ed. John Updike
Emily Dickinson, *Complete Poems*
Edna St. Vincent Millay, *Complete Sonnets*
May Swenson, *Nature: Poems Old and New*
Louise Bogan, *Blue Estuaries*
W. H. Auden, *Complete Poems*
William Butler Yeats, *Complete Poems*
A. E. Housman, *A Shropshire Lad*

My first pick is Virgil's *The Aeneid*, in the Robert Fitzgerald translation, which I reread recently, following on the heels of the C. Day Lewis version; Lewis tries to replicate the Latin line of sextuplets; Fitzgerald chooses iambic pentameter, which falls more naturally on the reader's ear. His postscript provides a wonderful insight into the narrative. (I haven't sampled the Dryden translation but have been told by Donald Hall that it is the best.) Why *The Aeneid*? Because, like a fruitcake, everything is in it: envy, lust, pity, family loyalty, love, uncontrollable rage, prophecy, and the inexplicable actions of the gods, which still act upon us in the form of government and luck. Also, it is delicious to read.

Now that we have The American Library, Whitman's *Selected Poems* and Shapiro's *Selected Poems* are on my list. Karl Jay Shapiro was a huge influence on my early life as a poet. He was the first "contemporary" American poet I read and the subject matter of the poems in *Person, Place, and Thing* almost took the top of my head off. "Buick," "Drugstore," "The University of Virginia" where "To hurt the Negro and avoid the Jew / is the curriculum" gave me permission to write about the real world I lived in, too. And I am old enough to remember when Whitman was shunted aside as wild, egotistical, and, gasp! a homosexual, therefore not worthy to be read.

On my list also, Emily Dickinson's *Complete Poems* and Edna St. Vincent Millay's *Complete Sonnets*—which, in my opinion, are the best Petrarchan sonnets written by an American poet, although Marilyn Hacker is not far behind. Let me add that when I was in college at Radcliffe, now defunct, subsumed by ever-greedy Harvard, Millay was scorned as sentimental, domestic, and came into the canon, when? In the '60s? So I have lived to feel justified in my ardor for her work.

May Swenson, who wrote all those years in the closet, only

toward the end of her life coming out as a lesbian, is responsible for some of the best contemporary love poems, encrypted in big-cat imagery for safety's sake.

After reading Auden I fell in love with form and from him I learned how to work in tetrameter.

Finally, a poet little read today: A. E. Housman. I know most of *A Shropshire Lad* by heart, having first encountered it as a lonely adolescent, a time when lugubrious melancholia and dying for love are especially attractive. Five years ago, recuperating very slowly from a nearly fatal carriage-driving accident, I re-memorized these poems from my dog-eared copy, which is small enough to fit in the palm of my hand, like a priest's breviary. I walked a mile slowly, eight times around our driving ring each day, while reciting "Bredon Hill," "Is My Team Ploughing," and "To an Athlete Dying Young." I think that having poems by heart not only, as I say to students who cannot imagine caring deeply enough about anything to go to prison for, provides you with an internal library to draw on in case you are taken political prisoner, but also plants those rhythms next to the heart where they thrum forever, systoles and diastoles of another life-giving system.

DAVID LEHMAN

Walt Whitman, *Leaves of Grass* (1855 edition)
James Joyce, *A Portrait of the Artist as a Young Man*
Ernest Hemingway, *Men Without Women*
T. S. Eliot, *The Waste Land and Other Poems*
Wallace Stevens, *Collected Poems*
W. H. Auden, *Collected Poems*
Arthur Rimbaud, *Illuminations*
Rainer Maria Rilke, *Sonnets to Orpheus*
Gertrude Stein, *Selected Writings*
Henri Michaux, *Selected Poems*
Frank O'Hara, *Lunch Poems*
Frank O'Hara, *Meditations in an Emergency*
Kenneth Koch, *Thank You and Other Poems*
John Ashbery, *The Mooring of Starting Out*

In making this list I have tried to be faithful to my recollection of the books that meant the most to me when I began to write poetry. Each of these titles made me want to write poems or gave me ideas for writing or taught me specific techniques that I could make my own.

In college, if asked to name a favorite poem, I might have said Eliot's "The Waste Land" or Keats' "Ode to a Nightingale." In graduate school I might have opted for Stevens' "The Snowman," Auden's "In Praise of Limestone," or Ashbery's "The Skaters." In my thirties I would have unhesitatingly declared Milton's "Lycidas" to be the greatest single poem in the language. Today? Well, Wordsworth's "Tintern Abbey" still brings tears to my eyes when I recite it, and Coleridge's "Kubla Khan" is sublime. Do I have to choose?

PHILIP LEVINE

John Dos Passos, *U. S. A.*
John Keats, *Poems and Letters*
Dylan Thomas, *Collected Poems*
Federico García Lorca, *Poet in New York*
Walt Whitman, *Leaves of Grass*
Yvor Winters, *In Defense of Reason*
William Carlos Williams, *Spring and All*
George Orwell, *Homage to Catalonia*
Cesare Pavese, *Hard Labor*
Juan Ramon Jimenez, *The Complete Perfectionist*, ed. and trans.
    Christopher Maurer
Fernando Pessoa, *The Book of Disquiet*

This is simply a list of eleven books that have been essential to me. Of course I could have extended it or substituted other books, but these popped out and demanded attention today. I put them in the order of my discovery and use of them. Most of them have gone on being useful for the duration.

Dos Passos created characters I already partly knew, but they were more adventurous in his world, more troubled, more desperate, more interesting. I loved these people, and I hated the country that betrayed them. With its newsreels and biographies and passages of poetry it read like no book I'd ever seen before. This was a modern novel, and I could understand it. I was 19 years old, and with Dos Passos' help I discovered I was of the modern world.

Poems and Letters is the most useful and inspiring book I ever read. Over the years the letters became more important to me than the poems; they showed me I could be who I was–a man very uncertain of what life meant and what my role in it might be–and still write my poetry.

Dylan Thomas was an early hero. No one sang the way he did; I was twenty-one when I found the work and fell in love with its density and drive. Did I understand him most of the time? Of course not. The music overwhelmed me and I thought, I've got to learn to sing, even a little. He took me back to Blake, where I remained.

Poet in New York by Lorca: The city, and all of one's shit-storm of feelings toward it, one's awe and rage and befuddlement, all of it belonged in poetry if you had the nerve to risk failure. Lorca was a map to the expression of my own sense of defeat by American capitalism as well as my determination to talk back.

"There is that lot of me and all so luscious," from Whitman's "Song of Myself," is the most useful single line I ever read. It may even be true.

With extraordinary intelligence and candor Winters takes apart most of the pretensions of the modernist critics in *In Defense of Reason*. He is the great curmudgeon of our poetry, wrong more often than right, but always useful in that he never pretends to know what he doesn't know, and he knows a lot. No one who ever lived was more serious about poetry. The prose is spare, precise, and barbed; a critic you can read. Every romantic should soak in this tub.

Williams' *Spring and All*: Here was the American language ungilded, raw, stunning, and the drive and energy that Americans put into their voices when their speech is driven by powerful feelings. As much as I loved recent English poetry–Dylan Thomas, Edward Thomas, Auden, Yeats, Hardy–and as much as I owed them, this work had to become part of the way I heard my language, my country, and my poetry.

Even in a corrupt world there are things worth fighting and dying for, there are people who do not sell out, there are causes that matter forever. *Homage to Catalonia* is a great book of hope, written in a prose style that any poet can envy and emulate. One of the monuments to the significance of citizenship in humanity.

I came to Pavese in my forties, read him only in English, and mainly in the William Arrowsmith translation, and although the settings are largely rural the poems resonated as deeply as any I knew. In my sixties he summoned me back to my origins. His feelings for landscape and the beasts and people who inhabit the landscape and are its flowers was the village counterpart to my Detroit. There's a marvelous new translation by Geoffrey Brock.

Having devoted fifty years to the attempt–often unsuccessful–to write poems, I discovered a book that indicated all was not lost. With humor, clarity, and savage intelligence, Juan Ramon makes the case for "a poetics of work." He answers some of the most profound questions facing a poet, and he does so with questions anyone might ask. A great book of wisdom that pretends to be nothing of the kind.

Pessoa is the finest companion one can have during the long years of loneliness that arrive after the age of sixty-five. He's made a brother of the solitary world, he lives in it with supreme sensitivity and tact. I've always loved Lisbon, but never so much as when I share its dark and secret corners with this poet.

LYN LIFSHIN

Sir Thomas Wyatt, *The Collected Poems*
Federico García Lorca
John Donne, *The Collected Poems*
Dylan Thomas, *Collected Works*
Emily Dickinson, *Selected Poems and Letters*
Sylvia Plath, *Ariel*
Robert Frost, *Collected Poems*
William Carlos Williams
The Bible
Walt Whitman, *Leaves of Grass*

These are not in any particular order of importance or chronology. I recommend Sir Thomas Wyatt, for his sense of the thought-being-thought-out, not overly polished and revised and revised and revised. I always loved the feeling of breath in his poems, the raggedness, the sense the words were rushing, hurrying, wildly racing to the surface. I love the breathlessness of a poem like "They Flee From Me That Sometime Did Me Seek":

> They flee from me that sometime did me seek
> With naked foot, stalking in my chamber,
> I have seen them gentle, tame and meek,
> That now are wild and do not remember
> That sometime they put themself in danger
> To take bread at my hand, and now they range,
> Busily seeking with a continual change...

I like the mystery here, the hint at darkness, the way the form does not intrude. I like the strangeness and how much is implied.

Read any collection of poems by Federico García Lorca. I love Lorca's incredibly beautiful use of language, his use of repetition, and the dream-like, flowing, magical sense in his poems. I think of two poems in particular. Firstly, "Lament for Ignacio Sánchez Mejías":

Cogida and Death

> At five in the afternoon.
> It was exactly five in the afternoon.
> A boy brought the white sheet

> *at five in the afternoon.*
> A frail of lime ready prepared
> *at five in the afternoon.*
> The rest was death, and death alone,
> *at five in the afternoon.*
>
> The wind carried away the cotton wool
> *at five in the afternoon.*
> And the oxide scattered crystal and nickel
> *at five in the afternoon.*
> Now the dove and the leopard wrestle
> *at five in the afternoon.*

I adore the sensuousness, the colorful language, how it is straight-forward yet seems to come from another world. The tension and sadness in this poem build up beautifully. Also, I love the story, the theater, and the sense of danger. The second poem I think of, which I love for many of the same reasons, is "Somnambulistic Ballad."

I admire John Donne for his playfulness, his metaphors, the changes his work went through from the early love poems to the later religious poems which seem to anticipate Gerard Manley Hopkins, always battling, always energetic.

I admire the metaphors in the love poems, poems like "The Bait." It starts off in a very traditional way but then there are leaps and mental twists. It begins:

> Come live with me, and be my love,
> And we will some new pleasures prove

By the end, the image of the fish and the bait twists the poem in various directions until the speaker becomes very different than the speaker at the beginning of the poem:

> For thee, thou need'st no such deceit,
> For thou thyself art thine own bait:
> That fish, that is not catched thereby,
> Alas, is wiser far than I.

The wit, the surprise, and the mental gymnastics are always interesting.

In later poems, such as "Sonnet XIV," Donne's use of argument takes on a more serious, less playful, attempt to debate, explore, discover:

> Batter my heart, three-personed God, for you
> As yet but knock, breathe, shine and seek to mend.
> That I may rise and stand, o'erthrow me and bend
> Your force to break, blow, burn, and make me new

I like the energetic rush of words, not unlike Wyatt. In fact, for my doctoral dissertation (which I completed half of) I traced a connection between Wyatt, Donne, and Dylan Thomas.

Like Lorca, I loved Dylan Thomas from the start. I suppose there is a dark mysteriousness in both poets that I am drawn to, as well as their incredible use of language. I know Thomas has been out of favor recently, but then, who hasn't at some time? When I began my master's thesis, he was my favorite poet. Now, he is one I admire for the strength and tightness of his formal poetry and the lushness of his more expansive poems. Like Donne, the acrobatics in his poems are dazzling. His language is rich, even gaudy, often strange, but always forceful and imaginative.

When thinking of Thomas, everyone probably thinks of "Do Not Go Gentle into That Good Night," "Fern Hill," and "Poem in October." I also recommend some of the shorter, tighter poems like "In my Craft or Sullen Art" that describes why he "labour(s),"

> Not for the proud man apart
> From the raging moon. I write
> On these spindrift pages
> Not for the towering dead
> With their nightingales and psalms
> But for the lovers, their arms
> Round the griefs of the ages,
> Who pay no praise or wages
> Nor heed my craft or art

I would recommend Emily Dickinson for her defying of the writing current during her life, for her unique leaps, and for her incredible ability to telescope and tighten her wonderful eccentricities. I recommend her for her toughness, dedication, her ability to leap, leave things out, work with abstractions as well as images, her intellectual richness, mystery— all make her so important. I like the sense of raggedness that appeals to me in Wyatt and Donne. More unique than her slant lines is her slant vision, her way of seeing is important to experience.

Because of Plath's life and early death, *Ariel* probably has been as widely read as any of the poets I've recommended. Even with the "myth" of Plath, I recommend her for her wonderfully startling poems that shock, amuse (they are often much funnier than on first reading) and her incredible leaps, energy, and daringness. I love the tightness of the poems in this collection, what is left out, the sexual openness and the leaps to a freeness. I admire so many: "Cut," "Ariel," "Lady Lazarus"– no one can forget the lines "Out of the ash / I rise with my red hair / And I eat men like air." Also so unforgettable: "The Tulips," "Edge," "Kindness."

I also recommend another somewhat out of favor poet, Robert Frost. The plainness of his language, the narrative quality, the use of language as it is spoken. I admire his ability to capture so much of New England in such a restrained, plain, forward yet musical way. I especially recommend some of his less popular poems.

I also recommend William Carlos Williams for his very clear and direct language, perhaps not popular right now but beautiful and haunting in its own way.

So much of the language in *The Bible* is very beautiful–its repetition, musicality. I recommend the Psalms from the Old Testament.

Something of Walt Whitman's probably also should be included for his free verse and rhythmic innovations, his multifaceted interests, and the range of his subject matter. *Leaves of Grass* shows his "thought-rhythm," his musicality, his emotion, and his strong feelings about love and sexuality.

I know if I were to make this list on a different day, I might choose different writers. Add others. But today, these are the ones that float up.

TIMOTHY LIU

FIVE BOOKS

If you want to be a great poet, then read five books of poetry a week for the rest of your life. That's what I overheard the Mentor say to the Young Poet over fifteen years ago. If you do the math (and the reading, as I have done), that's 3,900 books. So I will not be recommending specific poetry titles per se, but rather recall the infamous words of the late Joseph Campbell: "Follow your bliss!" What remains are a few books I have found to be indispensable companions on the journey toward the Promised Land, call it Parnassus or what you will. Some of these titles I have read over a dozen times, others just once. Each offers its own particular sustenance, its own kind of lastingness.

What is poetry without a consciousness of its own poetics? Can one imagine literature without theory? Not in any kind of responsible writerly way, only by way of enchantment found perhaps in one's readerly innocence once upon a time. As a primer, then, Roland Barthes' *The Pleasure of the Text* maps out the seductive relation between writer and reader that serves as the sublimated base for attentions to fixate upon: the art of the textual striptease. A cunning lingual foray into embodied pleasures. A quickie demonstration on how to shake that money-maker whether bedecked in prose or verse, inspiring all the nations to go a-whoring.

Hot on the heels of such wanton philosophy comes literary history to the rescue, the contextual *mise en scène* for the various performances of verbal debauchery. Octavio Paz's *Children of the Mire* documents his international travails through the landscape of belles-lettres. If I seem partial to disunited states, it's only as necessary antidote to the provincial epidemics of internalized xenophobia that have broken out on our Continent ever since its bloody founding. Now at the End of Wilderness, the trailhead's clearly marked: *Modern Poetry from Romanticism to the Avant-Garde*. These campfire chats, disguised as Charles Eliot Norton Lectures, bear resemblance to noble initiatory rites.

For further ruminations under an Abrahamic tent of stars, one only need contemplate W. G. Sebald's *The Rings of Saturn*, our author himself having been untimely ripped from our company and returned to cosmic dust *via la forza del destino*, alas. The past is too much with us, our Guide seems to say, as we follow him along the Eastern Coast of England, no longer sure just which world we are walking in. What remains is pure mystery, sentences as spells that conjure the sublime in a genre that has no name. A crash-course, then, in the Elegiac, the root of all poetic discourses that straddle the epic/lyric divide, time's horizontals endlessly derailed by a series of spirals whose verticality hurls us from the profaned mundane into some eternal realm.

If Sebald inhabits a world dominated by a masculine imagination, then surely Christa Wolf's *The Quest for Christa T* would offer a complementary portrait of a Guide who journeys by staying in place, East Germany in fact, imprisoned as it were by domesticity and a life cut short, the flow of cause and effect difficult to ascertain. *When if not now*? is the rallying cry throughout its pages, a contemporary summons to *carpe diem* not served to Marvell's Coy Mistress but to Shakespeare's imaginal Sister. And indeed, have we not all played Cinderella to the masked fêtes of Literary Society to which we have been denied formal invitation? How then gain access to princely Parnassus if its gates remain forever shut against us?

Simone Weil offers no glass slipper. She never even makes it to the ball. Hers is a time of ashes, not for herself alone, but for humanity. Hers is the Martyr's striptease, not of raiment but of the Flesh itself so that Spirit might eventually be reclaimed by the Bridegroom who never arrives, at least not in this life. *Waiting for God* transcends earthly ambition. It is the poetry of prayer itself, only to be answered in cloistered death. It puts vanity in its place, all books to be burned when the Earth is baptized with Fire. Poetry then will no longer be necessary. But until we can be brought back into the Presence, there must be those who have gone before us who can somehow show us the way.

GERALD LOCKLIN

Edward Field, *Stand Up, Friend, With Me*
Edward Field, *Variety Photoplays*
Charles Bukowski, *The Days Run Away like Wild Horses Over the Hills*
Frank O'Hara, *Meditations in an Emergency*
Sylvia Plath, *Ariel*
Norman Mailer, *Deaths for the Ladies*
Richard Brautigan, *The Pill Versus the Spring Hill Mine Disaster*
Ernest Hemingway, *In Our Time*
The Wormwood Review and *Poetry/L.A.*
The New American Poetry, ed. Donald Allen
Geography of Poets, ed. Edward Field

I'm limiting my selections to books since 1950 and presupposing that the reader will be concurrently pursuing a grounding in all the "greats" of the English language and in translation (or the originals) from other languages: Catullus, Wordsworth, Baudelaire, Li Po, Whitman, Dickinson, just to give an idea. My own consciousness is drenched with echoes from the poets I've taught for years in 20th Century British and American classes: Hopkins, Yeats, Auden, Dylan Thomas, Housman, Hardy, Robinson, Frost, Eliot, Pound, Stevens, Crane, Cummings, Jeffers, Roethke, W. C. Williams, Langston Hughes (and Ted), Gertrude Stein, etc. My list is also quite personal: poets and books which meant the most to me in my formative years, the 1950s and 1960s in particular.

Stand Up, Friend, With Me established, for me, absolute honesty and personal revelation as a source of power in poetry. *Variety Photoplays* established popular culture as a new mythology. In 1969, Charles Stetler and I published an article in *The Minnesota Review*, "Edward Field: Stand-Up Poet," that described what would come to be called the "Stand-Up" branch of postmodern American poetry (see the outstanding *Stand-Up Poetry* anthologies edited by my colleague Charles Webb, most recently from University of Iowa Press). Selections from *Stand Up, Friend, With Me* and *Variety Photoplays* are, of course, included in Field's *Selected Poems* from Black Sparrow Press.

Actually I could have named any and all books of Buk's from Black Sparrow Press but *The Days Run Away like Wild Horses Over the Hills* was the one that had the first major effect on me around 1970, although I already knew his work from *The Wormwood Review* and other little mags in which we were both publishing, he of course more prolifically than I. He was the quintessential poet of the spoken American language, especially as employed by the working (or unemployed) class. We became good friends and I have a book of memoirs, reviews, poems, and such: *Charles Bukowski: A Sure Bet*, from Water Row Press. Over 50 of his letters to me are housed in our library's Special Collections.

O'Hara, especially in *Meditations in an Emergency*, was the spontaneous, gestural poet with close links to Abstract Expressionism, the poet of the moment, the poet of free association (and Freud was rampant in the Village of those days). His *Collected Poems* has now been published, but I prefer my poetry in digestible portions.

I came to Plath's work through a poem, "Lesbos," in the *New York Review of Books* (I came to Field's "The Bride of Frankenstein" in the same tabloid). Plath was, by far, the best academic, confessional poet. She was freed by madness and impending suicide from her Ivy League training (with Lowell, especially). Her earlier work is conventional and labored, but she is also, if we must regard gender, the best American woman poet of her century. (I am not a great fan of Bishop, H. D., Amy Lowell, and such, although I'll admit to a weakness for Edna St. Vincent Millay.) Today excellent women poets abound. Lisa Glatt, Denise Duhamel, and Patricia Cherin are among my favorites.

Mailer's *Deaths for the Ladies* is a nearly unnoticed book from which I learned a lot about writing short poems.

The Pill Versus the Spring Hill Mine Disaster showcases Brautigan's troubled, but brilliantly tangential mind. Since the narrative and dramatic modes have resumed their places alongside lyric poetry, a lot can be learned from Brautigan's fiction too. My favorite of his novels is *A Confederate General from Big Sur*, about which Stetler and I published an unconventional article in *Critique* back in the day.

Hemingway remains my literary god. His best poetry was his prose (not his dadaistic early little-mag poems, although those exercise a certain fascination). My favorite novel of his, and perhaps of all novels, is *The Sun Also Rises*. Stetler and I published widely on his work in *The Hemingway Review* and elsewhere.

If they may be considered "books," I would add the bound, archived copies of *The Wormwood Review* (the best poetry magazine of the second half of the 20th century) and *Poetry/L.A.* (the best magazine of Southern California poetry during the same period, although with a much shorter run during the 1980s and early 1990s). As poetry editor of *The Chiron Review*, I aspire (along with my editor, Michael Hathaway) to approximate the eclectic excellence of those periodicals which were absolutely invaluable hosts to my own development.

If I were to select the two most influential anthologies of the period they would be Donald Allen's *New American Poetry* and Edward Field's *Geography of Poets* (and its sequel, *A New Geography of Poets*, co-edited (truth in advertising) by Charles Stetler and myself).

All of these poets were liberating influences on my work, as were "Howl" and the other early poems of Ginsberg.

THOMAS LUX

Hart Crane, *The Complete Poems and Selected Prose*
James Wright, *Collected Poems*
Theodore Roethke, *Collected Poems*
Charles Baudelaire, *Paris Spleen*, trans. Michael Hamburger
Josefa Heifetz Byrne, *Mrs. Byrne's Dictionary*
Primo Levi, *Survival in Auschwitz*
William Shirer, *The Rise and Fall of the Third Reich*
Barbara Tuchman, *A Distant Mirror*
Fyodor Dostoevsky, *Crime and Punishment*
Herman Melville, *Moby Dick*

  To do this I had to pretend someone put a gun to my head and ordered me to list 5-10 books that have been essential to me, as a poet. As a poet, and as a human being, this is the list I came up with. There have been hundreds of other books–poetry, history, natural science, novels, short stories, plays, biographies, general nonfiction, etc.–that have been and continue to be essential to me. Books not even published yet are essential to me. I can't wait, for example, for a new book by Bill Knott, Stephen Dobyns, Ted Conover, or Barbara Ehrenreich.

  I wore out several copies of each of the first four books during my twenties. I still read them and teach them today. As a young poet, I made a point of carrying poetry books around, partly out of affectation and partly because I read them all the time. The Crane and Baudelaire were particularly good because they fit easily into a jacket pocket. I loved Crane's poems before I had the slightest idea what he was talking about. The language, his rhythms, and the intensity of emotion were good enough. Later, as I learned a little more, I learned to love his poems enduringly. If the devil came to me and said "Tom, you can be dead and Hart can be alive" I'd take the deal in a heartbeat if the devil promised, when arisen, Hart would have to go straight into A. A. And then on to new poems!

  James Wright and Theodore Roethke: What do you say? Two poets so alive, so human, so passionate about their craft. They both do beautiful things with language and their poems move me deeply. I don't particularly want to be edified by poetry, or charmed, or mystified–I want to be moved, I literally want, and get when I go to the right sources, that feeling Emily spoke of: the feeling that the top of one's head is being taken off. I tried reading Crane once while shaving (testing Housman's theory) and nearly slashed my throat. Luckily, I had chosen a very dull razor.

Baudelaire! The first translations (I neither speak nor read a word of French) I read were 20 of the prose poems from *Paris Spleen* (I've seen that title translated in different ways), published in a little lavender paperback put out by, I believe, Cape Goliard. Michael Hamburger was the translator. Over many years, reading several other translations of Baudelaire, I still prefer Hamburger's. I read Enid Starkie's biography around the same time. An important message in these poems: life can be funny and tragic at the same time. In fact, humor can rescue, sometimes, the tragic and the tragic can give some weight to humor. Also, he teaches us the torment of money problems and to accept that we'll fall in love with the wrong people. We are complex creatures.

Mrs. Byrne's Dictionary: Its subtitle is "of Unusual, Obscure, and Preposterous Words." Any poet who would not like a book like this should have to turn in his or her poetic license. Not for obscure or fancy words or for showing off vocabulary but for the sheer joy and goofiness, and the wonderful onomatopoeic qualities, of so many of the words. The definitions are as much fun as the words themselves.

The next three books are history books. As Mr. Faulkner said: "The past isn't dead. The past isn't even past."

The last two are great novels. During the summer between my junior and senior year of high school I read almost all of Dostoevsky. Lord knows what I was thinking. I grew up on a farm. Maybe I took a tumble off a tractor as a child and hurt my head somehow. I didn't read *Moby Dick* until I was in my twenties. It's a poem, it's a paean, and it's the first American novel. I didn't mention them (except Emily tangentially) but both Dickinson and Whitman are essential to me as well. Emily and Walt are the grandmother and grandfather of American poetry. Melville (well, Mr. Twain too) is the grandfather of American fiction. On who is the Grammy of American fiction I will let others opine.

Read until you bleed.

J. D. MCCLATCHY

Virgil, *The Aeneid*
The American Heritage Dictionary
William Shakespeare

The Aeneid is undoubtedly the greatest poem ever written–lavish, psychologically acute, at once violent and elegant, sweeping and minutely worked, it is itself a classroom for the fledgling poet. Even as a schoolboy, working my way through the Latin, I could marvel at the intricacies of the poet's manner. Later, I admired Virgil's creation of a tone, the *sfumato* effect of sadness, a sadness that is neither grief nor weariness. All poems are about memory, and here is the best of them–memory's intolerable system of weights and releases, the screech owl beating against the shield.

The appendix to *The American Heritage Dictionary* (especially in the first edition), with its fascinating index of Indo-European Roots, lays out the family connections of individual words in a way that reveals the secret life of language. The origins and mechanics of metaphor are all here. I'd recommend too a good thesaurus, useful not for finding the words you want but for eliminating those you don't. And for those whose temperament inclines them to rhyme, a rhyming dictionary (the Merriam-Webster is a solid choice) helps one past the brain's monosyllabic inertia.

More than any other texts, the plays of Shakespeare fired my sense of the possibilities of language. The level of poetic invention, in service to the dramatic instinct, was never higher. An impossible standard, of course, but a constant wonder and spur.

It is crucial for any young poet to immerse himself in the collected works of the titans, first in order to imitate them shamelessly, then to chip away at their encrusting marble to find the figure of his own imagination. Usually, one starts neither with the ancients nor one's contemporaries, but with the modern masters: Yeats, Eliot, Stevens, Auden. From each there are incalculably valuable lessons to learn, and with luck those lessons will cancel out each other, leaving a chastened but informed imagination. Among more recent poets who will best reward close study–that is, show powerful solutions to old literary problems–are Robert Lowell, Elizabeth Bishop, and James Merrill.

American poets need early on to school themselves in the true ambitions of the American imagination. The scripture here is the essays of Emerson, exuberantly enigmatic, endlessly challenging. From Emerson everything flowed, and our necessary poets–from Whitman and Dickinson to Frost and Robinson–are required reading. Soul-making is the poet's task; these writers gave us its terms.

PETER MEINKE

Fyodor Dostoevsky, *The Idiot*
Anton Chekov, *Selected Stories*
Gustav Flaubert, *Madame Bovary*
Flannery O'Connor, *Collected Stories*
Kingsley Amis, *Lucky Jim*
John Donne, *Selected Poems*
John Keats, *The Poems and Letters*
William Butler Yeats, *The Collected Poems*
Howard Nemerov, *Selected Poems*
Richard Wilbur, *Selected Poems*

When I was young, I was drunk on Russian novels, particularly Dostoevsky, but also Tolstoy, Gogol, and Turgenyev. *The Idiot*, with its tragic mix of idealism and evil, is still vivid to me, perhaps because my Army commander restricted me to barracks when he found it on my bunk in Würzburg, Germany, thinking (correctly) that it was a subversive book (this was 1956, when Russian tanks rolled into Budapest). Later, in a direct line, I began reading Chekhov's short stories and plays; and over the years have used them in my writing classes as exquisite examples of understatement and the power of subtle but specific observation. Recently I visited St. Petersburg and was enormously moved when Dostoevsky's apartment by the canal was pointed out to me. The immensity of Russia explains a lot.

I have always read a lot of fiction, and still do. *Madame Bovary* seems to me to be a perfect book, and the subject of the conflict between romantic longing and reality is one that I often touch on in my poems and stories.

Flannery O'Connor's savage satire and poetic sentences were great teachers, as was Kingsley Amis' ribald humor in *Lucky Jim*. Perhaps because of these fiction writers, much of my poetry, even in the dark poems, is touched by humor: they showed me how deeply ingrained and complex comedy can be. A book with no laughs in it is a long book indeed–and not very true to life.

Perhaps all the fiction that I've read has influenced the kind of poetry I like to read and write: poems with stories that are accessible but mysterious at the same time; poems with ambiguous endings, and lines full of strong rhythms and clear imagery. In short, I like lyric poetry with a narrative thrust, and hope that my poems have the same dramatic interest that stories do.

The first poet with a major influence on me has those qualities. A wise teacher at Hamilton College, after looking at some of my gushy undergraduate poetry, told me to go buy *The Selected Poems of John Donne*. It was great advice, and I still love Donne's mixture of wit and passion, and his formal dexterity. The title poem of my most recent book, *The Contracted World*, is modeled on Donne's "The Sun Rising." And John Keats' poems and letters have always made me marvel at his precocious genius: "I am certain of nothing but the holiness of the heart's affections and the truth of imagination..." is a sentiment close to my own core beliefs.

When I started memorizing poetry, I began with William Butler Yeats: strange poems like "Who Goes With Fergus?" and "The Song of Wandering Aengus," as well as the well known ones like "The Second Coming." To me, he's the greatest poet of modern times; I don't try to learn from him, exactly–I just read him more or less constantly, for enjoyment, and hope some of his example rubs off.

I did learn a lot from Howard Nemerov, because I wrote my Ph.D. thesis on him; I liked him for his Donne-like qualities brought into the 20th Century, and I read him backwards and forwards until I felt I knew why he ended a line here, why he broke a stanza there, etc. I wrote the first long study of him, published in the University of Minnesota's "Pamphlets on American Writers" series. His dark poems are always intelligent, often hilarious; and they never bored me.

The last poet on my list, Richard Wilbur, is of course still writing, but I've always loved his seemingly effortless way with formally beautiful poems, and the generosity of his mind (as shown, for example, in "The Writer"). We know it isn't effortless, but his seamlessness is what Yeats must have meant when he wrote, "Yet if it does not seem a moment's thought / Our stitching and unstitching has been naught." And I admire the example of Wilbur's life itself, though I've only met him a few times. He seems to be leading a stable, creative, open and generous existence, which is what I hope for in myself as I head into the winter years. I should perhaps add that, without at all detracting one iota of what I said about these ten wonderful writers, the list I write tomorrow could be quite different.

E. Ethelbert Miller

Langston Hughes, *The Big Sea*
James Baldwin, *The Price of the Ticket*
June Jordan, *Things I Do in the Dark*
Carolyn Forché, *The Country Between Us*
Cornelius Eady, *you don't miss your water*

THE ESSENTIAL BOOKS OF A TAMBOURINE MAN

I live in a house full of books. Four floors of volumes have accumulated over the years. One of the more difficult decisions I've had to make recently is deciding which books to discard or give away. Maybe I'm entering a mid-life crisis. I know I can't save or keep everything. I just don't have the space. The thought of placing a book in the trash was never a thought I could make room for. Last year I donated hundreds of books to two charter schools in the Washington, D. C. area. These books I felt were no longer *essential* to my collection. Some were children's books purchased when my children were at the scratch and sniff stage. Others were economic and education textbooks, computer manuals and novels that were never made into movies. The primary focus of my personal library is African American culture. Quite a number of my books are autographed. I consider them to be precious jewels and a measurement of wealth and information. When I compile a list of books that aided me in my development as a writer it's not something that has to stay too long on the stove. I can easily select five books that are important to me. But first let me mention a few songs and musical compositions that comprise my personal soundtrack. In many ways certain songs led me to become a writer. I don't think I would have become a poet if it wasn't for the lyrics of Paul Simon, Bob Dylan, and Phil Ochs. Long before I was studying the Harlem Renaissance and the poetry of Langston Hughes and Countee Cullen, I was humming lines from "Mr. Tambourine Man" on a New York subway.

I wanted to write like Dylan. "Mr. Tambourine Man" was almost an anthem for me. I was young and restless and the words wrapped around me like a harmonica's wail. "Let's forget about today until tomorrow." In almost every Dylan song there is a line or two that sticks in your head and it's crazy and profound and you can't forget it. That's what forced me out of the house one day in search of a guitar. I purchased one and the only song I learned to play was Simon & Garfunkel's "The Sounds of Silence."

I wasn't writing poetry in high school but I was discovering music. I was one of fewer than a hundred African American students that attended Christopher Columbus High School. My friends were mostly Jewish and with the Vietnam War going on we often found ourselves drifting around Greenwich Village on the weekend. With the war came the music of Phil Ochs. While black kids were getting into Motown I was singing "Do You Believe in Magic?" in the shower. This song by the Lovin' Spoonful might be the only song I know all the words to. I didn't embrace Soul music until college. Going south to Howard University was a migration of consciousness. I was introduced to the poet laureate Smokey Robinson by way of Michelle Calhoun. She was a cousin in his family and the woman I would eventually marry. Her love of songs like "My Girl" would find a place in my heart long before I saw the movie *Cooley High*. At Howard University my soul was also saved by jazz and the saxophones of Pharoah Sanders, Archie Shepp, and John Coltrane. It was my literary mentor Bob Stokes who gave me jazz albums as well as books in the early seventies. He wanted to insure that after I graduated from college, I would graduate to a better sound of music. If you walked past my first apartment you would have heard Johnny Hartman singing "I Just Dropped by to Say Hello." Bob had suggested I listen to Hartman and maybe this is why I wrote mainly love poems during a time when black poets were angry and talking primarily about revolution. The classic love song for me is "For the Love of You" by the Isley Brothers. That was my summer song of 1974. The poet Ahmos Zu-Bolton and I toured the southern part of the country reading our poems in places like Tuskegee, Alabama, Alcorn, Mississippi, and Galveston, Texas. Ahmos was in love with a woman in Houston and I couldn't keep my mind from thinking about Charlene back in D. C. There is no better song to listen to on the car radio at night while thinking about the person you love. If you hear "For the Love of You" it's a way of God placing his hand on the back of your head.

What about books? I don't think I would have thought about becoming a writer if I hadn't read *The Big Sea* by Langston Hughes. In my memoir, *Fathering Words*, I wrote the following:

> Langston Hughes did not live in Cook Hall. I was the only poet in a dorm filled with future doctors, lawyers, preachers, teachers, government workers, musicians, dentists, soldiers, lovers, drug addicts, crazy Negroes, Muslims, Republicans, gays, and guys who would see you every day and not speak. It was not the best place to become a writer. I should have left Howard like Langston left Columbia. Would I have thrown my books into the ocean?

The Big Sea introduced me to the writer's world. The second part of Langston Hughes' autobiography also contains a good eyewitness account of the Harlem Renaissance or New Negro Movement. This was all new to me. At Howard I was introduced for the first time to the tradition of African American literature. Reading about Hughes and then walking across Howard's campus and meeting someone like the poet Sterling Brown will make you think twice about going to law school. I only thought about it once. I was also introduced in college to James Baldwin. I remember my brother and sister reading *Another Country* and *Giovanni's Room*. They were older than me so I saw Baldwin's books as belonging to them. It didn't matter since I would be attracted more to Baldwin's essays. *The Price of the Ticket* is where you find all of them. I seem to always be going back to this book in search for a quote or just to remind myself about what the Civil Rights Movement was all about. I'm living in America and what does this mean? Baldwin explains things for me better than Martin Luther King, Jr. or Malcolm X.

When I fell in love with the poet June Jordan, I knew what the Isley Brothers were doing when they were not singing. Many of June's "hit" poems can be found in *Things I Do In The Dark*. I laugh every time I read about Miss Valentine Jones. She's the real Miss Black America. I remember when the book was published in 1977. I happened to be staying in June's Brooklyn apartment when the box came. We opened it, celebrated, laughed and had wine. I think we called Alice Walker who lived a few blocks away. Maybe this is my favorite book of June's because it contains her first love poem to me. June's voice and politics shaped my development as a young writer moving from twenties to thirties.

In the 1980s I started writing numerous poems about events taking place in Nicaragua, El Salvador, and Chile. In Washington I read at political and cultural gatherings with Roberto Vargas and Ariel Dorfman. My work reached out to countries I had never seen. Poems found their beginnings in the eyes of friends and the pauses in conversations. I was living in the Adams Morgan neighborhood of Washington and interacting with people from Central and South America. Carolyn Forché's *The Country Between Us* was a model for my new work. I wanted to write poems like "The Colonel." This was the first real haunting poem I had ever read. Today whenever I see a picture of a hostage or a prisoner of war with a black bag tied over his head I think of Forché and the ending to her poem "The Visitor" which she wrote in 1979: "There is nothing one man will not do to another."

When I started thinking about writing my memoir and trying to remember things about my father, Eady's *you don't miss your water* was the emotional rock I climbed. When I read this book in order to write a blurb I could feel the honesty and pain on every page. I learned so much about the relationship between men from this book. The theme of family has been a major one in my work the last few years. This book by Eady was a key to a door hidden inside my heart. Even the way he wrote about his sister helped me to explore my own sister's voice in *Fathering Words*.

What is *essential* is that a writer always remember the beginning of things. Writing is a way of not forgetting. It might take a few more years to determine what new books (or songs) will become essential to my growth.

I hope to remain humble as I continue on my creative and spiritual journey. Right now I'm listening to Alicia Keys and she is singing "You Don't Know My Name." So it was in the beginning, so it shall be in the end.

THYLIAS MOSS

Philip and Phylis Morrison, *Powers of Ten*
Felice Frankel and George M. Whitesides, *On the Surface of Things*
Galway Kinnell, "Saint Francis and the Sow"
Jorge Borges, *Ficciones*
Howard Nemerov, "Style"

How difficult it is to think of five to ten essential titles. Perhaps it is the word "essential" that challenges me so thoroughly. I don't feel that I've read enough books to know of all books available, which ones are in fact the essential ones.

But what follows are books for which my passion seldom wavers. These I place back on the shelf–my library's in the basement–only to have to run down the stairs to locate something in them. Maybe it's just I love to run my fingers along the spines of books, the pleasure of identifying the book that will contain information that, because of the ritual of selection, begins to seem like a reward. Here goes:

Powers of Ten is a book about scale in which anything can become the center of the universe, a journey, that beginning with the most familiar scale, the back of the hand right before your eyes, moves in both directions, into the cells of the hand, each time by a magnitude of ten, the magnification accessing an interior landscape and universe almost impossible to believe that a hand contains. The journey can be magnified the other way, of course, expanding by magnitudes of ten the external landscape and universe until arriving at the limits of the macrocosm as those limits may presently be determined. Part of my delight with this journey is the simultaneity of activity on all scales at once, and anything being the center of that; anything in the microcosm, simply by advancing by a magnitude of ten can lead to something all encompassing. I like the outward thrust toward conversion. I like the confirmation of connectedness. From the furthest reaches of existence, it is possible to access the interiors of the atom of a single piece of my genetic material. Perhaps I experience an ultimate belonging. Or maybe I just like this cosmic address, being somewhere in the Virgo Cluster of galaxies and yet my hand being located in that, the middle of the middle of the middle. So much holds us.

I chose *On the Surface of Things* maybe because I have been known to feel some despair (that didn't deserve to be called despair) over having to supply depth to something I wanted to think about or write about; maybe because I wanted to defend the surface that was being so maligned, and that was becoming untouchable, I was drawn to this book—just its cover was irresistible to me. I was told not to dwell on the surface of my topic, but I began finding it impossible not to dwell there. As I delved and plunged, I found not the depth I was supposed to find, but more surface. Each level, once I encountered it, became more surface. The surface is too easily dismissed, yet that is where so many interactions occur. I cannot kiss, for instance, but that surfaces come together, surfaces that when magnified reveal patterns and crinkles in which tiny particles reside, my surface also a world for the unseen. Light interacts with surfaces. Rainbows form as light interacts with surfaces of water in the air. The rainbow in the oil in a puddle on the surface of the sidewalk is interacting with light as well; the top surface of the oil interacts directly with light while simultaneously the bottom surface of the oil interacts with the top surface of the puddle. This book celebrates surfaces, exposes some surfaces not regularly considered. The reprieve of the surface!

Read any book, all the books, in which "Saint Francis and the Sow" by Galway Kinnell appears. No other poem has tempted me to plagiarize; but I resisted, writing instead an essay, "Contemplating the Theft of the Sow." It is that bud in the poem, not that it is a bud, but that it "stands for all things," much as the cell, the center of the atom in a single cell of my hand stands for all things when that cell is opened up by powers of ten to reveal the universe. And so does Kinnell's bud open, "for everything blossoms," everything opens to access that universe. I'm glad Kinnell wrote that down, for as I dwell on surfaces, I am likely to forget to explode the kernel, a likelihood Kinnell suspected, also writing in the poem that "sometimes it is necessary to reteach a thing its loveliness," those words unforgettable, reteaching me each time I think of them, read them, or see a bud that is anything, exploding its surface to access the surface of the blossom.

This circle of thought of course takes me to Borges, his *Ficciones* that explode interactions with appearances, accessing where surfaces of imagination interact with surfaces of realities. His surfaces consistently are entrances to more surfaces. The explosions explode. Then, I'm no longer sure that there is a surface at all or anything as supportive or trustworthy as that. The debris of explosions somehow self-sustains, and if I am to be comfortable, I'll have to be comfortable with that.

I am comfortable with it perhaps because of a poem by Nemerov, "Style," in which on the surface it appears that two great books did not get written, and yet, the surfaces of the ideas that would have been the substance of the books, one of them "about nothing," when navigated explode into a difficult greatness, tenuous as greatness should be, the exploded possibilities of those ideas circling in my thinking, unseen pages writing themselves, their surfaces filling with words that for not being written are better than real pages sinking into and becoming lost in the depth that the printed words pull them into.

I guess I should stop here, in the depth of words.

NAOMI SHIHAB NYE

Henry David Thoreau, *Walden Pond*
Jack Kerouac, *The Dharma Bums*
William Stafford, *The Way It Is*
William Stafford, *Writing the Australian Crawl*
William Stafford, *You Must Revise Your Life*
W. S. Merwin (every book)
Robert Bly, *Silence in the Snowy Fields*
Harryette Mullen, *Blues Baby*
The Other Voice: Twentieth Century Women's Poetry in Translation,
        ed. Bankier, Cosman, Earnshaw, Keefe, Lashgari and Weaver
Ruth Ozeki, *My Year of Meats*

In addition to *Walden Pond*, Thoreau also wrote poems, which I may like more than he did. He never felt his poems were what he wanted them to be. There was one which ended, "The wind that blows / is all that anybody knows." As a teenager, I loved that and pinned it to my bedroom door. In eleventh grade, I felt *Walden Pond* to be the most crucial reading discovery I had ever made. Here was an eloquent book which confirmed a life on the eccentric edge, the fringe, without material gain as a major driving force, as being an honorable life too. *Walden Pond* heightened my sense of devotion to things that mattered, i.e. writing, reading, solitude, simplicity. I wish high school classes still read the entire book. Now I think most curriculums only include an excerpt, since many students found this book too slow or boring for their tastes. I never felt alone again after I had read Henry.

Well, I simply could not have lived without Kerouac. He was the second man I had been waiting for. We have the same birthday. Unfortunately he had already died when I discovered his books. But I became friends with his wife Stella and she was a very precious woman. (Met his cats too.) *The Dharma Bums* was the first book of his I ever read, then went on to read everything, including what other people wrote about him. Often I thought they had missed the true essence somehow. *The Dharma Bums* confirmed something about spontaneity which was critical to me as a college student and young poet. The academic life often felt very stiff and TOO OFFICIAL. I had not one moment of desire to go on to graduate school after completing four undergraduate years, though I loved my university. Kerouac balanced out the energies. I always said to myself that Henry got me through high school and Jack got me through college and I still feel that way. Whether they would have liked one another in real life, I have no idea. Maybe.

Stafford's earlier collections, all of which are utterly essential to so many lives, are contained in *The Way It Is*, a marvelous, large, posthumously published edition from Graywolf Press. The book also includes many pieces which were unpublished at the time of his death. Whenever you need a compass, go here. Whenever you need a voice that tunes you back to whatever you most need to hear, open this book and feel the guidance coming in clearly. The same can be said for *Writing the Australian Crawl* and *You Must Revise Your Life*. These great volumes from Ann Arbor's Poets on Poetry series are companions for life. I have used these collections of comfortable, endearing, challenging Stafford essays as a text in many classes and whenever I run into people from those classes, they often say, "Those books never found the shelf yet!"

Read any book ever written by W. S. Merwin. I cannot name only one because they are all essential. If you have not read Merwin's work, basked in his work, lived with his work, let his work filter into your seeing and your silence and your breath, get with it.

I know, I know, *Silence in the Snowy Fields* is a very old book, and I have loved many of Robert's later books, but this one gave me so much as a young poet and I would not want anyone to miss it now just because it came out a long time ago. It is very pure, very clarifying, like a filter.

Mullen's *Blues Baby* is a re-issue of a book called *Tree Tall Woman* (with some additions) by a highly original, delightful, STUNNING voice. I used to share poems from this book with my students in early writers-in-the-schools workshops and saw how the energy of the poems sparked so much energy in young writers. Harryette's recent *Sleeping with the Dictionary* was a finalist for both the National Book Award and the National Book Critic's Circle Award.

Find *The Other Voice* anthology if you can! Perhaps it is out of print but I wish every teenage girl in this country could have a copy. My copy is totally marked up with love notes in all the margins. The voices of Arab and Jewish women stand out in profound parallel harmony and power, but all of the voices are indelible.

Ozeki's *My Year of Meats*, is a quirky and absolutely terrific novel. What this book brings to light, regarding current culture and the actions that pass as "okay behavior" between humans, and between humans AND animals, is nothing short of masterful.

ED OCHESTER

~~~

Edward Field, *Stand Up, Friend, With Me*
Edward Field, *Variety Photoplays*
James Wright, *The Branch Will Not Break*
James Wright, *Shall We Gather at the River*
Frank O'Hara, *Lunch Poems*
Neruda and Vallejo, ed. and trans. Robert Bly
Gerald Stern, *Lucky Life*
Gerald Stern, *The Red Coal*
Philip Levine, *The Names of the Lost*
Judy Grahn, *The Work of a Common Woman*

This list is in chronological order of reading.

Field's use of pop materials–movies, urban legends, headlines, etc.–and his courage in using "loose" longer narrative lines knocked me out. And charmed me.

Wright's use of "the deep image" and his rootedness in the blasted landscape of Ohio (read: America) was deeply moving to me, as was his ability to convey compassion without emotional sloppiness or sentimentality.

Well, sure O'Hara–dozens of things to like. Most of all his invention of "the present progressive" in some of his poems. And his use of "ephemeral" personal details (a lot of poets still don't know that everything about life is ephemeral–that understanding is what underlies both comedy and tragedy–as in, say, *King Lear*). And his cockiness. And, like Field, his use of contemporary materials. Here was a poet who didn't set his poems in never-never land or write only from European vacations!

Bly's *Neruda and Vallejo* was my introduction to two great poets, and to the idea (I was very young) that great contemporary poems were being written in languages other than English. I love everything about Neruda, most of all his political commitment and his hatred of the George Bushes of this world, for whom power and money are obviously more important than individual human lives.

Stern's allegiance to the individual, and his poetry of meditation (it's almost all poetry of meditation) have been very important to my own practice.

Once again, Levine's non-sentimental compassion for the poor and the lost–wonderful echoes of Whitman–attracted me to his work, and this book contains some marvelously complex linkages of past and present that have been conscious/unconscious models for some of my work.

Like Bukowski, Grahn's skillful use of extended narrative about contemporary characters and events has been both pleasurable for me and influential on the shaping of my own poems.

Many of my favorite poems by these poets are characterized by grace and wit (in the 16th and 17th century sense, as in some of Donne's conceits) rather than "heavy" and more philosophical pieces *a la* Hart Crane or Berryman. Oh well, for those I'll go back to Keats and Shakespeare (the plays, not the shorter poems).

MOLLY PEACOCK

Gaston Bachelard, *The Poetics of Space*, "Drawers, Chests, and Wardrobes"
Elizabeth Bishop, *Collected Poems*, "The Waiting Room"
George Herbert, *Collected Poems*, "The Pulley"
Philip Larkin, *Collected Poems*, "Church Going," "Talking in Bed," and "Days"
Robert Lowell, *Collected Poems*, "Skunk Hour" and "Epilogue"
Charlotte Mew, *Collected Poems*, "The Trees Are Down"

All the books listed above I read in my twenties and still embrace with the joy and anxiety of meeting a trusted friend from whom I've been separated by circumstance. Will it be the same? And it always has been, at every meeting, for decades now.

If you are intrigued by the psychological implications of interior spaces, from tiny spaces such as a toy box to larger enclosed spaces such as attics and basements, then *The Poetics of Space* by French philosopher Gaston Bachelard will hold you in its capable but whimsical hands. This is a talisman book for me, one I return to again and again, not so much to completely re-read as to thumb through. You can read it the way some people read a Bible, randomly pointing a finger to a page. Wherever you land, you'll find a curious, illuminating, psychological idea to locate you in a new mansion or hut, or a cottage or a castle of thought.

"Why not say what happened?" Elizabeth Hardwick asked Robert Lowell as he struggled to write around a personal subject. To answer her, he wrote directly, and began to forge a way of writing that broke open the poetics of the last half of the twentieth century. "Epilogue" is a poem that directly addresses the terrors and pitfalls of saying "what happened." But "Skunk Hour" is an exercise in consonants, Anglo-Saxon language use updated to our current tongue, trespassing in its vocabulary, and redemptive in its final image of the skunk who "jabs her wedge-head into a cup of sour cream / and will not scare." It fortifies me every time, and reminds me that whenever an animal suddenly appears in a poem, the true self of the poet has stepped forward and we meet that poet, soul to soul.

Isn't it often the case that the best self of the person who is the poet comes forward in the work? I love many poets whom, I'm sure, I'd hate to sit next to at a dinner party, and Philip Larkin is one of those. But it's not his social being that inhabits his poetry. Instead, brimming in the poems is the private, lonely, unvarnished, grouchy man struggling to live in opposition to accepted norms, and working with a linguistic muscularity that seems incongruous with the 98-pound-weakling persona he projected. I read "Church Going" for the way Larkin redeems the full power of adjectives in phrases like "this accoutred frowsty barn" and "a tense, musty, unignorable silence" of the church. "Talking in Bed" displays a gloriously negative equation in its finale when Larkin looks for words "not untrue and not unkind" and "Days" tries to answer the unanswerable question "What are days for?" in only ten lines.

Virginia Woolf called Charlotte Mew "the greatest living poetess"; and Thomas Hardy wrote, "Miss Mew is far and away the best living woman poet who will be read when others are forgotten." Ironically, Mew is so utterly forgotten that you can't even buy her *Complete Poems* in the United States (though it is available in England and Canada, published by Penguin). She's uneven and didn't leave us a huge body of work. No American would call her "major." But I think Mew is the foremother of our current style of lyrical narration, or narrative lyric. I love her poem "The Trees Are Down" because of the "wish" and the "crash" and the "rustle" of the felling and because of the shocking image of a rat beneath them. Mew is utterly conversational but completely rhythmical when she says "I remember thinking: alive or dead, a rat was a God-forsaken thing, / But at least, in May, that even a rat should be alive." She allows us to enter her consciousness, to share with her the horror at the destruction of the great plane trees at the end of the gardens, and she is even bold enough to invite us to hear the angel of Revelation at the end. Her poem is protean and alive—and tree-like in its look and in its long-limbed construction.

But my ultimate favorites, then and now, are Elizabeth Bishop and George Herbert, whom Bishop loved as well. I love Herbert for his passion and utterly human attachment to God, so visceral and whimsical, and Bishop, too, for her visceral whimsy. My favorite of Bishop's is "The Waiting Room" for the child's eye, knee-level view of the waiting room full of "arctics and overcoats, / lamps and magazines." I always find Herbert's "The Pulley" thrilling because of its plays on the word "rest." In that poem, God has a "glass of blessings" which he pours out for us, but he keeps "rest" away from us, leaving us longing. There is a kind of longing in Bishop's poetry as well that seems to connect with this, a restlessness, a search I identify with as a poet. It was a longing for something deep, intense, yet made of the ordinary—something I feel in both Herbert and Bishop—that brought me to poetry in the first place.

LUCIA PERILLO

C. K. Williams, *Tar*
Elizabeth Bishop, *Collected Poems*
Cesare Pavese, *Hard Labor*
James Wright, *The Branch Will Not Break*
John Berryman, *Dreamsongs*
Louise Glück, *The Wild Iris*
Larry Levis, *The Widening Spell of the Leaves*
The Norton Anthology of Poetry

Tar: This book is where I started. It made me, a failed fiction writer, realize the narrative possibilities–coupled with speed, and therefore exhilaration–of poetry.

I know Elizabeth Bishop by the smaller version of her *Collected Poems*, rather than by individual books, because she wrote relatively few poems. She made me understand that the narrative can be sedate also.

Hard Labor: Pavese shows me how the narrative can move in its barest-boned way, by removing my familiar cultural elements.

The Branch Will Not Break: Somehow Wright is the truest American, and there is something seductive in the stupid sentimentality of the deep image poets.

Dreamsongs: Because we need to be reminded about rhyme too.

The Widening Spell of the Leaves: Levis is Wright's true heir, and the contemporary writer I now think is most likely to enter history, though when he was living I did not understand his poems.

Some of the books that were important to me when I was younger (like Sharon Olds' *The Dead and the Living*) have fallen from my interest. But probably such a list exists imaginatively always in flux–it is a differential equation–and this is why exercises like making lists are intellectually entertaining but always inaccurate.

Many of the poets to whom I go back often (like Yeats and Dickinson) I know through their whole body of work and not through individual books. For this reason I keep the *Norton Anthology* by my desk, and though I thought the Norton was boring when I was younger it is now the book that I would least want to be without.

I realize that this is a pretty conservative, dead-white-guy list, but it is also an accurate reflection of where I am–at least this week.

CARL PHILLIPS

Emily Dickinson, #520, "I started Early–Took my dog–"
John Donne, *Holy Sonnets* (all of them)
T. S. Eliot, "The Love Song of J. Alfred Prufrock"
George Herbert, *The Temple*
Homer, *The Iliad*
Herman Melville, *Moby Dick*
Frank O'Hara, "To the Harbormaster"
William Shakespeare, Sonnet #129, "The expense of spirit in a waste of shame"
Sophocles, *Oedipus Rex*
Walt Whitman, "I Saw in Louisiana a Live-Oak Growing"

"I started Early–Took my Dog–" is one of those poems in which Dickinson charges a simple enough scene with the erotic, and shows how the overwhelming power of the erotic is its own divinity, at once threatening and glamorous. The poem suggests that we all have a bit of the urge to surrender, to yield to abandon, once we get away from the fettering safety of "civilization."

Donne is one of the most persuasive religious writers because he is so willing to declare his own difficulty with belief–he is also one of the most carnal writers, which makes me trust him all the more: I know he lived. And it is largely from Donne that I learned the power of syntax to attract–syntax as a form of Eros.

Eliot's "The Love Song of J. Alfred Prufrock" shows the struggle to live as an individual in the midst of a society that distrusts and fears individuality–and the way in which society more often than not succeeds at crushing the spirit–that's what Eliot is getting at. What lesson is more important than that? Eat the peach.

The Temple contains all of Herbert's poems in the order he chose for them. Read in order, the poems are a daring sequence that tracks the struggle between two kinds of devotion, the sacred and profane, and refuses to compromise private yearning in the name of public expectations. And there's simply no poet more versatile, in terms of form, than Herbert.

The Iliad is nothing short of a meditation on what it means to be alive, it is so much more than an epic poem–it encompasses the lyric and narrative genres, comedy and tragedy; and I find there's no human emotion or gesture that Homer has overlooked. I still weep at the scene where Hector's infant son plays with the plumes on Hector's helmet, this the last moment that the boy will see his father alive. It's a rare poignancy that can move us so many centuries later.

Moby Dick is the American epic, or at least it has epic range and an inventiveness that anticipates postmodernist genre-fusion. Somehow, in the vast space that lies between chowder and cetology, the darkness of the human psyche gets hauntingly illuminated. And somehow, this is also a rollicking tale of the adventure that unfolds, or can, when innocence meets experience.

In O'Hara's "To the Harbormaster," who is the harbormaster? God? A lover? Whoever he is, the speaker has failed, once again, to serve as he knows he ought to and, in fact, wants to. What I love here is the speaker's trust in the flawed vessel of the body. The poem is a refracted valentine of sorts, an apology that isn't entirely sorry. Surely one of the loveliest poems–and truest–in English.

Shakespeare's sonnet #129 is syntactically dazzling–the way in which the 12-line sentence countered by the sentence of one couplet enacts the disparity between our understanding of lust, and our inability to keep it in check despite our understanding. It speaks to the truth of lust, and of lust as one of our most ineradicable truths.

Riddles are at the root of *Oedipus Rex*, and we learn that living is itself a riddle for which all of our rational thinking is ultimately no match. The answer to the sphinx's riddle was, of course, Man. But the riddle that haunts the play is the one never answered: What is Man?

"I Saw in Louisiana a Live-Oak Growing" is a powerful, poignant, clear-eyed look at that part of love that at once includes and transcends the sexual–a resonant affection, and the need for it, not just between men, but between any two human beings, though what makes the poem especially important to me is its insistence on "manly love," the love between two men. How daring for Whitman to have said so back then. And how important, still.

ROBERT PINSKY

Emily Dickinson, *The Complete Poems*
The Odyssey of Homer, trans. Rieu, Fitzgerald, Lattimore, Fagels
William Faulkner, *The Hamlet*
Francis Fergusson, *The Idea of a Theater*
Aristotle's Poetics, ed. Francis Fergusson
James Joyce, *Ulysses*
Wallace Stevens, *The Collected Poems*
English Renaissance Poetry, ed. John Williams
William Carlos Williams, *The Collected Poems*
William Butler Yeats, *The Collected Poems*

The anthology *English Renaissance Poetry* is the most concentrated source I know for the essential nature of the sounds of English in verse, especially in certain poems by Ralegh, Greville, Jonson, Gascoigne, and Donne. From the University of Arkansas Press, the anthology is based on Yvor Winters' three-part essay published in *Poetry* magazine in the late thirties.

I think lists should be personal, idiosyncratic, tentative. Efforts to make a definitive "canon," as professors in each American generation have done, are doomed to the second-rate and the quaint.

Young poets should strive to make a personal list, based on admiration and resistant to fashion.

CHARLES POTTS

Fyodor Dostoevsky, *The Brothers Karamazov*
Alexander Lowen, *The Physical Dynamics of Character Structure*
Oswald Spengler, *Der Untergang Des Abenlandes (The Decline of the West)*
Arnold Toynbee, *The Study of History*
Carl Sauer, *Seeds, Spades, Hearths, and Herds*
William Wordsworth, "Ode: Intimations of Immortality from
    Recollections of Early Childhood"
William Shakespeare, *King Lear*
Dante, *The Inferno* from *La Divina Commedia*, trans. Charles Singleton
The I Ching
Leonardo da Vinci, *The Artabras Memorial Edition*

    There being so many great books in the world, the challenge to select ten essential ones brings into play the greatest plasticity language offers us in its infinite capacity to be distorted, deleted, and generalized upon. What gets left out may be equal in our own minds, let alone the minds of others, to what gets left in. Each book by each author also implies, in most instances, the rest of that author's work, to say nothing of the works of others to which it can organically be related.

    I can only begin with the book, and the author, which kept me from going any crazier than I otherwise did during high school, Fyodor Dostoevsky's *The Brothers Karamazov*. There is only one novelist on my list though his prophetic work ringingly associates itself in my psyche with his three nearly exact in intent peers, Herman Melville, especially *Moby Dick: or The Whale*, D. H. Lawrence's *The Rainbow Trilogy*, and Emily Brönte's *Wuthering Heights*. Dostoevsky remains the premier entry on my list because no other novelist with whose work I am familiar knew as much about how people are put together. How does human life work its way out in our "selves" and the other people we share the planet with?

    Alexander Lowen, perhaps the premier living psychiatrist, has made many contributions to human understanding. In *The Physical Dynamics of Character Structure*, originally published in 1958 and available now in paperback as *The Language of the Body*, Lowen quotes Dostoevsky as often as he quotes Freud. Building on the work of his mentor Wilhelm Reich's *Character Analysis* (whose *The Function of the Orgasm* ought to be on somebody's short list of the greatest books [Ed. note: See Clayton Eshleman page 54]), Lowen brings the indispensable human body into the picture of a healthy psyche where only the mind and its discontents had reigned for so long. Midway in my life, in my thirties, I more or less abandoned fiction in favor of psychology as the fastest way to understanding human behavior and character. I used to offer a year's supply of fiction repellent with every subscription to *The Temple*, our poetry magazine. Other psychologists worth anyone's time are Richard Bandler's *Using Your Brain for a Change* and Fritz Perls' *Ego, Hunger, and Aggression*, published in Africa in 1942.

Oswald Spengler's two volume work *The Decline of the West* is lavish in its use of two other great German writers, Goethe and Nietzsche. Frequently dismissed as a pessimist and certainly a fatalist, I recited the title of Spengler's work in German because I've learned to lean on the literal where it matters, i.e. *Der Untergang des Abenlandes* literally reads *The Going Under of the Evening Lands*. The West doesn't exactly decline in Spengler; it goes sideways, and has been doing so according to Spengler since Wellington's victory over Napoleon at Waterloo in 1815. To test that opinion politically, ask yourself what in American history is remotely equivalent to the adoption of The Bill of Rights, an attempt to codify some high points of the Enlightenment, as a counterweight to the spuriously inspired Constitution in the late 18th century? Spengler can be windy and the short way out of that is H. Stuart Hughes' succinctly titled volume *Oswald Spengler*, where Hughes delineates the essential Spengler and describes it correctly as "history as literature."

Arnold Toynbee, British author of the six volume *A Study of History*, once considered abandoning his work because he mistakenly thought that Spengler had already done it. Later he learned to dismiss Spengler's excesses in favor of his own. Together they are the yin and yang of world history (not considering China): one a German fatalist who is actually wildly optimistic, Dionysian undoubtedly, about the new cultures growing often clandestinely in the carcasses of the old; and the other the British empiricist who holds out the hope that with sufficient intelligence at the helm disaster can at least be postponed if not held off indefinitely. Other than Toynbee, the only other writer I have read who speaks of Spengler does so dismissingly, the Canadian philosopher Marshall McLuhan, whose *Understanding Media* isn't on my short list but would be if it were much longer. For China, see Joseph Needham's multi-volume *Science and Civilization in China*.

Fiction gives way to psychology which folds into history which is superseded by geography in the person of Carl Ortwin Sauer, author of *Seeds, Spades, Hearths, and Herds*, published by the MIT Press. Carl Sauer founded the geography department at the University of California at Berkeley, and brought back into the fore the neglected, comprehensive study of human activity. His life work in the volumes, *Sixteenth*

Century North America, The Early Spanish Main, Seventeenth Century North America, and Northern Mists, is a geography of the North American continent at the time of the European incursion written with primary focus on the contact documents. Sauer is cited as one of the must reads by Charles Olson in his *Bibliography on America for Edward Dorn*. Olson, who   recommends saturation as a way to mastering subject matter, has only snide things to say about Toynbee, the man who saturated history. Sauer saturated geography and his observation that we "must take the risks of interpreting the meeting of natural history and cultural history..." is the place I continuously return when I feel like I'm losing my bearings.

Of the three great poets whose work most intrigues me, William Wordsworth's "Ode: Intimations of Immortality from Recollections of Early Childhood" seems to me to have been written in that queasy no-man's-land between cultural history and the pining for nature or natural history and the recognition by the poet that there is no way back to that reputedly marvelous time when humanity was part of nature, before we became, in the hints of Jarred Diamond, chimpanzees with a gene for speech, i.e. "Though nothing can bring back that hour / of splendour in the grass, of glory in the flower." The Ode is a poem of course and not a book, although Wordsworth wrote many books. He is one of the few authors I admire whose complete work I've never been able to read. The later poems, *The Prelude, The Recluse*, set my teeth on edge. They seem predictable, stodgy, safe, what poets write when they can no longer write poetry, something unfortunately that has happened to droves of American poets with dozens of books and barely a line or two of actual poetry. It won't make American poets sleep any better at night to realize that there is more poetry in Charles Francis Atkinson's translation of Spengler than there is in the complete works of all but a handful of American poets.

The pinnacle of poetry in English is William Shakespeare of course and the pinnacle of Shakespeare is the tragedy of *King Lear*. It is almost as if the natural condition of at least English human nature, as if it were a separate kind, is nuttiness and how it might be coped with. It gets us back to where we came in, the great crazy gestures of Dostoevsky's characters, all the way back up through the rent in the soul Wordsworth first expressed.

We will only escape and then only temporarily on the spiritual path. *La Divina Commedia* deserves its place as one of maybe three apexes of world literature. I thought I was angry until I read Dante. And stick with Charles S. Singleton's "prosy" translation. Attempting to put Tuscan terza rima into English terza rima is an undoable bad joke, especially when the rimes are slanted.

The I Ching is the basis of Chinese civilization and I've spent decades of my life looking for antidotes to the failure of western civilization. *The I Ching* is one such antidote, and as both Confucianists and Daoists find their origins there, the functional equivalent of the Old Testament.

Book ten on my list is one I've only come across recently although it is hardly a new book. I stumbled onto the work of Leonardo da Vinci almost by accident, looking for famous and successful bastards to round out a hammer lock I was intending to put on some loose ends from my childhood. I spend hours contemplating his fabulous perspective. I published a poem once in *The Temple* by Zoa Smith, a fine poet with whom I was privileged to share the stage one night years ago at the Nye Beach Writer's series in Newport, Oregon. Zoa Smith's poem is entitled "Paging Leonardo," and it too is about his earth shaking perception and perspective. For visual artists, whom I only know by association, it must all be about perspective, where do I see the subject from, from where do I intend the viewers of this work to see it, and how do I want them to react? Where is the vanishing point? For musicians working in the auditory mode, the key is the signature, the time frame, the measure. For writers it must be point of view or angle of attack. How, from among the infinite possibilities, am I going to present the work and what effect do I intend to have upon whom with it? How deal with the interplay of subject and theme?

Lowen and Sauer are the only Americans on my list. I'm a citizen of the earth far more profoundly than I am a citizen of the United States. I suspect I've either read, published, or listened to as many poets as any person my age, some of which I dearly love, especially the twenty-five whose books I've published. Writers can only write what they know, and then only if they have sufficient discipline to find something out. I lament, re-reading this, the dozens of writers who have helped me comprehend the world whom I've not mentioned, none perhaps any more than Ford Madox Ford whose neglected classic *Parade's End* has to be in here somewhere.

DONALD REVELL

Ezra Pound, *The Cantos*
John Ashbery, *The Double Dream of Spring*
Hart Crane, *White Buildings*
Robert Creeley, *For Love*
The Book of Common Prayer (liturgy of the Episcopalian Church in
     America)
Henry David Thoreau, *Walden*

These are the books that have mattered most to me. From Pound
and Ashbery, I have read to learn size and inclusiveness, to study
expansiveness and nourish the ambition to be entirely human in every
line. From Crane and Creeley, I have read to learn concision, accuracy,
tact and the ecstatic powers of reticence. From *The Book of Common
Prayer* I have learned cadence and the reason for All of the Above. And
in *Walden*, my daily reader and missal, I study to reverence the silences
surrounding all writing, all reading, all prayer.

ADRIENNE RICH

James Baldwin, *The Price of the Ticket: Collected Non-Fiction 1948-1985*
Muriel Rukeyser, *The Life of Poetry*
Howard Zinn, *A People's History of the United States*
Ben Shahn, *The Shape of Content*
June Jordan, *Some of Us Did Not Die*

None of these is a book of poetry. A poet should read a great deal outside of poetry. All these books are by people who have struggled to think about the world as they knew it.

Baldwin is one of the great American novelists and essayists.

Rukeyser's *The Life of Poetry* is an essential text on the significance of poetry in social crisis. To be read and then reread.

A People's History of the United States: Not to know this history is to be unmoored as a poet and a citizen.

The Shape of Content: A great artist on the making of visual art and its social function.

In *Some of Us Did Not Die*, distinguished poet, teacher and activist, Jordan gathered her remarkable essays on things happening in her neighborhood and in the world.

HARVEY SHAPIRO

Charles Reznikoff, *By the Waters of Manhattan*
George Oppen, *Collected Poems*
William Carlos Williams, *Selected Poems*
Thomas Wyatt, *Complete Poems*
John Donne, *Complete Poems*

There are books I don't want to comment on that I think essential for any writer or reader: *The Bible*, the epics of Homer and Virgil, Shakespeare's plays. But these are the culture's choices, I believe, not my individual choices. This anthology is based on the sound assumption that every writer has his own small shelf of essential books, books that he or she will turn to when the world doesn't make sense, or language no longer makes sense, or the idea of writing a coherent line of verse seems like a dream of Eden.

I remember when I was teaching at Bard College in 1949 and William Faulkner came to speak. In the course of his talk he said that every year he had to reread *The Book of Job*, *King Lear*, and *Moby Dick*. You can see how those books would help provide him with both the rhetoric he needed and a vision of the human condition.

Anyway, here's my own idiosyncratic list.

Charles Reznikoff's *By the Waters of Manhattan*. This selection of his work, published by New Directions, was made by George Oppen, or so Oppen told me, and I believe it remains the best introduction to his work. I think Reznikoff's poems are essential for the way they can clear the head, open the eyes, enable one to see the urban landscape clearly. His poetry is a lesson in how to discard the lyric ego when it becomes an impediment to vision. He is like a saint or Zen master or Hasidic master teaching you humility. You feel he honors people, places, things for their own selves; he doesn't see them as material for his rhetoric, as say Robert Lowell does in his late sonnets.

George Oppen's *Collected Poems*. Oppen's work has been a mainstay for me, and, I suspect, for many other poets, because of its integrity, honesty. As against what he calls "A ferocious mumbling, in public / Of rootless speech" he sets down his words with such quiet conviction, a conviction born, you feel, out of hours of contemplation, a lifetime of quiet thought, so that there's no denying their reality. It is, to quote him again, a "truthfulness / Which illumines speech." You believe in his words and you believe in the world those words point to: "The small nouns / Crying faith / In this in which the wild deer / Startle, and stare out."

William Carlos Williams' *Selected Poems*. At this point I should say that I'm obviously not ranking poets. I don't believe that Williams is a greater poet than, say, Yeats or Wallace Stevens. I go back to Yeats and Stevens often but only when I have a specific appetite for them. Yeats' dramatic gestures (all his poems are dramatic gestures) can be cloying. Stevens can be too rich in rhetoric. These poets are not daily bread for me the way Williams is. I feel his language is as close as we can get to an adequate language for our time.

There are two more books on my shelf–the complete poems of Thomas Wyatt and John Donne. I go back to Wyatt because he's so close to the very springs of English poetry, the first great English poet you can read without thumbing back to the glossary. And he can write a very pure lyric line, make a sweet sound (Oppen used to love his work). When the woman speaks in his poem "They Flee from Me" and says "Dear heart, how like you this?" you have a voice in your ear that has traveled through centuries. Amazing. John Donne I need because he can raise plain speech, the language of conversation (his conversation, of course) to the level of music. He can begin with a spoken line and then so amp it up that at the end of the poem you think what you've heard is symphonic.

With these five books I think you can build a world.

RON SILLIMAN

William Carlos Williams, *The Desert Music*
The New American Poetry, ed. Donald Allen
Jack Spicer, *Book of Magazine Verse*
Jack Spicer, *Language*
Robert Creeley, *Pieces*
William Carlos Williams, *Spring and All*
Louis Zukofsky, *"A" 22 and 23*
Robert Grenier, *Sentences*
Kathy Acker, *The Childlike Life of the Black Tarantula*
Barrett Watten, *Plasma / Paralleles / "X"*
Charles Olson, *Proprioception*
Henri Lefebvre, *Dialectical Materialism*

THE DECISIVE BOOKS IN MY LIFE

"What does not change / is the will to change"

What do I mean by this list? The books that follow are not necessarily "the best" or even "most important" from the perspective of literary history, although each is a superb work in and of itself. Nor are these books necessarily my favorite writing, even by these very authors. Rather, these were the books that were for me "essential" in that, in each instance, the work forced me to rethink and redefine what I was doing as a poet, writer, even as a person. Often, this had as much to do with *when* I read them as anything else. Always, it had to do with what each taught me. These then are the books that changed me.

The Desert Music

It was through this book, and especially its title poem, that I first truly discovered poetry and understood that I would some day be a poet. I came upon this volume quite by chance in the Albany Public Library when I was a junior in high school, spending a weekend morning reading, avoiding the chaos of a household with a mentally ill adult. It was, I swear, the oddity of a hardback with pale yellow binding that first drew me to the book.

I'd been writing fiction for six years and was beginning to recognize that I would be a writer, although only with the foggiest and most grandiose notion of what that might mean. I'd been unhappy with my fiction as well because what I was interested in most in my own writing seemed to have little if anything to do with elements of character or plot. But what I could not see was how I might get at this thing–I wouldn't have called it the sensuality of language because I simply didn't have the vocabulary for that then.

Suddenly, reading Williams' words aloud, I realized that I didn't have to struggle for this unnamed object of desire because *here it was*, absolutely clear, utterly present. Williams depicts a figure asleep on the bridge between El Paso and Juarez and asks:

> How shall we get said what must be said?
>
> Only the poem.
>
> Only the counted poem, to an exact measure:
> to imitate, not to copy nature, not
> to copy nature
>
>
> NOT, prostrate, to copy nature
>   but a dance! to dance
> two and two with him –
>   sequestered there asleep,
>   right end up!

Ironically, it was Williams' most narrative poem that led me to see a possibility for writing that extended well beyond vulgar narrative.

The New American Poetry

I attended–more as a teen party crasher than a serious writer–the Berkeley Poetry Conference in 1965 and spent the rest of that year and all of 1966 getting to know the poetry that was included in Donald Allen's breakthrough anthology, *The New American Poetry*, around which that conference had been organized. In addition to Allen Ginsberg and Jack Kerouac, the two contributors who'd already broken through into a broader public awareness in the United States, the Allen anthology first made widely available many other poets who would become the foundation for a generation of literature–John Ashbery, Paul Blackburn, Gregory Corso, Robert Creeley, Edward Dorn, Robert Duncan, Larry Eigner, Barbara Guest, Le Roi Jones (now Amiri Baraka), Kenneth Koch, Denise Levertov, Michael McClure, Frank

O'Hara, Charles Olson, Jimmy Schuyler, Gary Snyder, Jack Spicer, Phil Whalen, and John Wieners just for starters. Over four decades later, the Allen anthology–as everybody I knew called it–remains a touchstone of just how breathtakingly good an anthology can be. The number of writers in the Allen who did *not* go on to have major publishing careers and profoundly impact the next several generations of poets can be counted on the fingers of one hand.

However, because it sold over 100,000 copies, Allen's imperfections have had lives of their own. The volume's single most audacious move, which was to divide its 44 poets into five "divisions" or "groups"– Allen uses both words in his preface–has proven as troubled as it was inspired. One of the groups is a hodge-podge, a second–the so-called San Francisco renaissance–is largely a fiction and the one person who could have provided some continuity to that cluster was awarded to the Black Mountain poets. Yet the next two generations of poets would take these divisions much more seriously, which, among other things, kept them (us) from asking why the Objectivists are missing from this volume. Their inclusion would have made for a more radical as well as more historically accurate collection.

Book of Magazine Verse and *Language*

I discovered the work of Jack Spicer when Shakespeare & Co. Books in Berkeley, where I'd been participating in a weekly open reading series, decided instead to devote one Sunday afternoon in early 1966 to a memorial reading for this poet around what would have been his 41st birthday. The reader was someone of whom I'd never heard before either, Robin Blaser. But the work connected with me in ways I could not account for just from listening, so I went hunting for Spicer's books. In 1966 (and for much of the ensuing decade), there were really just two that were readily available and each was profoundly unsettling.

Language, first published in 1964, was a book that at first felt impossible within the world of the New American poet. To begin with, it insisted on a concept of language for the poem that was not ignorant of linguistics. This meant that all the claims that Olson in particular and the projectivists in general were making about the ear and breath suddenly sounded quaint, romantic, even mystical. Yet in its arms-open-wide embrace of loss and despair, Spicer sounded a completely different note, one that demanded a larger emotional palette for the poem than was being used by the New Americans. In *Book of Magazine Verse*, published right after his death, Spicer made explicit the degree to which he understood his poetry as an active intervention of the literary scene, figuring the book as a book of "typical" (sometimes comically so) poems that might appear in various periodicals, ranging from *The Nation* to *Downbeat* to *The St. Louis Sporting News* to *Poetry Chicago*. *Book of Magazine Verse* is the forerunner of all the critical poetries now being written, from the work of Bruce Andrews to that of Brian Kim Stefans.

Pieces

In the creative writing program at San Francisco State in the late 1960s, the students were almost all passionate followers of the New American Poetry, differing only in *which* of its identified trends they considered the "correct" path for poetry. The bulk of the students I knew seemed devoted to various modes of Black Mountain poetry–Olson, Duncan, Creeley, Levertov, Blackburn, Eigner, Dorn et al. As students, we took the theoretical pronouncements made by Olson and Duncan very seriously. So when Edward Dorn and LeRoi Jones both made breaks–Dorn with his comic opera pseudo-epic philosophical tome *Gunslinger*, Jones with his immersion into black nationalism via (this was always the hard part to figure out) Maoism, they were perceived by many as prodigals. But when Creeley took just as radical a turn in *Pieces*, one could not explain the process away so easily. Here was a major New American demonstrating that Olson's dictum that "What does not change / is the will to change" must also be a personal commitment.

I and my friends should have seen it coming. Already, Creeley's previous book, *Words*, had moved away from the romantic neo-Beat lyrics of *For Love* towards a poetic that was more formal and looking directly to Zukofsky in its sense as to what form might mean for the poem. But the poems in *Words* still basically looked like poems, or close enough to what we knew as poetry, to fool us into seeing continuities rather than development and departures. With *Pieces*, however, you could not make the same mistake:

> Here, there,
> every-
> where

As early as the 1950s, Creeley had written on the question of referentiality, but it was not until *Pieces* that his work began to demonstrate what a post-referential work might mean.

Spring and All

In 1970, Harvey Brown's Frontier Press published what may have been a pirate edition of William Carlos Williams' 1923 book, *Spring and All*, a work that embeds some of Williams' most famous early poems, including "red wheel barrow" and "The pure products of America," within a booklength theoretical manifesto, one that defines poetry as "new form dealt with as a reality in itself." That remains, 80 years after its initial publication, the most concise and accurate definition of the poem I have ever read. The book reveals Williams to have been more than equal to the critical challenges of modernism and shows him to be operating on a level at which among his peers only Pound or Stein could even hope to aspire.

Yet in 1970, *Spring and All* had been out of print for more than 40 years, having barely received any distribution or notice at the time of its original publication. Its reissue literally stunned the community of poets in the San Francisco Bay Area. Overnight, Olson's theoretical writing no longer seemed the latest thinking. But it was especially appalling to discover that somebody had gone beyond *Projective Verse* decades before Olson had written it. More than any other volume, this book convinced many poets in my generation that we had to go back and look at the early modernists all over again and that we couldn't trust the general wisdom.

"A" 22 and 23

What was the single finest volume of poetry in the 20th century? At least in the U. S. and in English? For my money, it's one of the next two items and you can take your pick. The first is Louis Zukofsky's final work on the long poem *"A."* Written in the early 1970s, some years after his wife Celia presented Zukofsky with the choral collage that is the poem's concluding *"A" 24*, these two poems, each composed around a five-word line, offer us as perfect a balance as anyone has ever achieved of verbal density with lyric richness:

> Late later and much later
> surge sea erupts boiling molten
> lava island from ice, land
> seen into color thru day
> and night: voiced, once unheard
> earth beginning idola of years
> that love well forget late.

The five-word line offers a substantial range of metric and syntactic possibilities and Zukofsky takes advantage of every one as this single sentence demonstrates. The text moves between lucid exposition and material opacity almost phrase by phrase, *idola* (false images) precisely to the degree that we imagine words as transparent, as access to things. Tale and tone are open to anything here, from this creation myth to the most moving poetry written on the death of JFK to Zukofsky's signature obsession with all matters domestic, *"A" 23* concluding literally with an alphabet that leads to the street on which the poet's son, violinist Paul Zukofsky, then lived: *arbutus.* I think of these two works—each roughly 30 pages in this small format—as twin poems and today can see how they not only bring the great long poem to closure but further connect *"A"* to *80 Flowers*, Zukofsky's final sequence of dense lyrics (and itself a greatly underrated masterpiece).

Like several of the works in my list, it is virtually impossible now to find *"A"22 and 23* in its original format. In each instance, however, that format was an important contributor to the overall power of the reading experience. For the next item, any other format strikes me as unthinkable.

Sentences

When Robert Grenier came to the University of California at Berkeley to teach in 1969, his poems already were telescoping down from the post-Lowell lyrics (still visible in his first book, *Dusk Road Games*) with which he had originally gone to Iowa City for his graduate degree. Influenced now by Stein, Zukofsky, and Creeley, Grenier was seeking the poetic equivalent of sub-atomic particles: what might make language work? Was it actually possible to capture consciousness at the very instant in (and through) which it became language? This quest led Grenier to start a magazine with Barrett Watten entitled *This &*, in its initial issue, to declare, all in caps, "I HATE SPEECH." That was a calculated overstatement, of course—Grenier was obsessed with the spoken as well as the written—but he wanted to identify a language for poetry that was not *déjà toujours* already encased within the confines of speech as *genre*.

As Grenier filled up notebook after notebook, it seemed unclear how these notes, some of them just verbatim transcriptions of snatches of conversation, might eventually be transformed into poetry. Indeed, with the exception of what we would now call language poetry journals, like *This* or *Tottel's*, Grenier's own publications of poetry were relatively few until, following a show in a gallery setting at Franconia College, Whale Cloth Press published *Sentences* in 1975. *Sentences* was a book in a box: 500 cards, 5 inches high, 8 inches wide, text typed (in "landscape" format) in Courier from an IBM Selectric typewriter, housed in a dark blue cloth covered folding box. Not only could one shuffle the cards, there was a rumor that no two boxes had started with the works in the same order.

More important than the presentation was the content. One example:

JOE

JOE

One could hardly find, or even imagine, a simpler text, yet it undermines everything people know or, worse, have learned, about titles, repetition, rhyme, naming, immanence. If we read it as challenging the status of the title, then on a second level it is the most completely rhymed poem conceivable. And vice versa. As language, this is actually quite beautiful in a plainspoken manner, the two words hovering without ever resolving into a static balance, never fully title and text, nor call and response, neither the hierarchy of naming nor parataxis of rhyme.

There were, of course, other, earlier works that focused on the micropoem, such as Aram Saroyan's books in the 1960s. Where Grenier differed was in his persistent focus, insisting that the poem's responsibility first of all was to the language through which it came into being. So where Saroyan had one or two poems per book that actually expanded what poetry might do, *Sentences* had hundreds.

Sentences was originally published in an edition of only a few hundred copies. Today an electronic edition is available from the Whale Cloth website, but otherwise this seminal work has never been reprinted. I keep my copy literally next to the *OED*.

The Childlike Life of the Black Tarantula

In 1973, Kathy Acker was writing and self-publishing this novel one chapter per month, handing out individually bound chapters each month at readings around San Francisco. Indeed, these short pamphlets listed their author only as The Black Tarantula, a persona Acker used during much of that period. The only woman in San Francisco that year to have a crewcut, Acker came across as the essence of punk generation extremism, although once you got to know her–a woman whose book crowded apartment included parrots named Art and Revolution and hamsters or guinea pigs named Cage and Mac Low, you realized that the persona was exactly that–a protective shell than enabled Acker extraordinary freedom as both individual and artist. When you read the chapters, already stamped with their distinctive genre formula of *plagiarism + pornography = autobiography* and realized that this was not a con but an attempt to re-invent fiction from the ground up, the bravery of it as a writing project just made your jaw drop.

I use the word *plagiarism*, which Acker did as well, especially after she was sued by a hack novelist, but in reality what Acker did was to appropriate texts in ways that foregrounded their social presumptions. In this sense, she carried the use of found materials beyond the primarily combinatory functions found, say, in early works by Jackson Mac Low to a mode that has more in common, say, with the films of Godard or the murals of Diego Rivera. To this material, a second layer of discourse derived from the most exploitive modes of porn was superimposed, a method that allowed Acker to approach and address the abusive conditions of her own childhood. Thus, in fact, she could write a work that was, at one level, precisely about the construction of the master tropes of fiction, such as character, while in the same moment presenting autobiography almost in its purest form.

While Acker's genre was always fiction, her use of the devices of writing as a primary mode of intellectual investigation made her an integral part of the poetry community, especially in San Francisco. From her and Grenier, in particular, I learned that one must be willing to go exactly where your vision leads you, even if that place seems not to exist or otherwise be impossible.

Plasma / Paralleles / "X"

I've been influenced by every book Barrett Watten ever wrote, including *Radio Day in Soma City*, but the one that has had the greatest impact on my own writing, the one I'm still apt to find myself reading in a dream, is this Tuumba Press chapbook from 1979. In it, Watten uses a combination of syntax, surrealism, and philosophical investigation (both with and without the caps) to arrive at a New Sentence entirely different from anything any other of my peers had ever written. The opening passage of "Plasma" is as powerful as anything I have ever read:

> A paradox is eaten by the space around it.

> I'll repeat what I said.

> To make a city into a season is to wear sunglasses inside a volcano.

He never forgets his dreams.

The effect of the lack of effect.

The hand tells the eye what to see.

I repress other useless attachments.   Chances of survival are one out of ten.

I see a tortoise drag a severed head to the radiator.

They lost their sense of proportion.   Nothing is the right size.

He walks in the door and sits down.

It gives me shivers just to type that up. Watten here has arrived at a space in which the referential content of the language can be seen clearly for the machinery that it is. Rather than draining syntax of its power the way, say, Clark Coolidge's long poems from this same period do, Watten underscores the grammatical imposition of drama. All three of the pieces in this collection work, to one degree or another, from the same principles, demonstrating that the most investigative and intellectually demanding writing can employ all the devices of fiction without ever surrendering to them. If for me the lesson of Grenier's *Sentences* was how to hear the phrase and how to recognize the beginning, middle and end of even a single vowel as separate moments in the poem, *Plasma / Paralleles / "X"* taught me how to read within the sentence as a dynamic architecture. That's a lesson I use every day of my life.

Proprioception & Dialectical Materialism

The first of these two volumes is the most schematic of Charles Olson's critical writing, the second a translation of an early (1940, but written in '36) book by the French philosopher of everyday life. The first appeared originally as a chapbook in Donald Allen's Writing series from Four Seasons Foundation, the second in the same Nathaniel Tarn-edited Cape Grossman series that first published Zukofsky's *"A" 22 and 23*. The Lefebvre was not translated into English until 1968, Olson composed his series of notes in 1961 and '62. Olson may have read or heard of Lefebvre, possibly through Tarn, but it's certainly not a given.

I've joined these two books because it was their conjunction, rather than either one individually, that puts them on this list. I found myself reading the two of them more or less at the same time, scratching my head at Olson's insistence that thinking takes place within the body, following Lefebvre's attempt to rescue Marx for a western Marxism that was only then starting to emerge when it became clear to me, utterly and completely, that these two books were making, with different vocabularies and working out of radically different intellectual traditions, *the same argument*.

It's an argument about the nature of knowledge & knowing, that the first can never be present without the second being simultaneously active, so that knowledge itself can never be decontextualized and certainly can never be static. As Olson puts it, "that *movement* or *action* is 'home.'"

It is within *Proprioception* that Olson, so often characterized as the poet of voice & breath, offers his note on "Logography":

> Word writing. Instead of 'idea writing' (ideogram etc). That would seem to be it.

Olson goes on to situate the origin of phonetics in the function of naming. Whether or not this is good historical linguistics, I couldn't tell you, but what to me is/was the most fascinating side of this extraordinary process is the degree to which it reveals Olson pursuing the consequences of his ideas *even when* it turns the poet on his head, right side up. There is an ambition within Olson's critical writing that is never more overt than here, a confidence that the simplest focus on a particular, any given detail, how, for example, a word is sounded, can, if you just follow it out, take you *anywhere*, and that nothing in turn can be the restricted domain of the expert.

Similarly for Lefebvre, identifying a Marx that is the furthest thing from the static intellectual dictator that Stalinism sought to turn him into, a Marx that in the 1960s and '70s will become visible to those who begin not with *Capital* or *The Communist Manifesto*, but with the *Grundrisse*, *The Eighteenth Brumaire of Louis Bonaparte*, and *The German Ideology*, which transform the role of theory within the political.

Finally, this leaves me with the question of *what about all the other books*, all the other titles that have similarly had a profound impact on me both as person and writer. Here, simply to acknowledge some, are a few that I have found very nearly as defining as any I've listed thus far: Rae Armantrout, *Extremities*; Roland Barthes, *Writing Degree Zero*; Walter Benjamin, *Illuminations*; Charles Bernstein, *Controlling Interests*; David Bromige, *My Poetry*; Clark Coolidge, *Polaroid* & *The Maintains*; Robert Duncan, *Roots and Branches* & *Bending the Bow*;

William Faulkner, *As I Lay Dying* & *Sound and the Fury*; Lyn Hejinian, *My Life*; Roman Jakobson, *Six Lectures on Sound and Meaning*; James Joyce, *Ulysses*; Claude Lévi-Strauss, *Tristes Tropiques*; David Melnick, *Eclogs, PCOET,* & *Men in Aïda*; Herman Melville, *Moby Dick*; George Oppen, *Discrete Series, This in Which* & *Of Being Numerous*; Bob Perelman, *7 Works*; Ezra Pound, *The Cantos*; Thomas Pynchon, *V* & *Gravity's Rainbow*; Jerome Rothenberg (ed.), *Revolution of the Word*; Ferdinand de Saussure, *Course in General Linguistics*; Gertrude Stein, *Stanzas in Meditation* & *Tender Buttons*; Ludwig Wittgenstein, *Tractatus Logico-Philosophicus* and *Philosophical Investigations*.

W. D. SNODGRASS

Walt Whitman, "Out of the Cradle Endlessly Rocking"
Henri Coulette, "The War of the Secret Agents"
Thomas Hardy, "Afterward"
Short poems by Ezra Pound, Sarah Cleghorn, and Ruth Soter
Randall Jarrell, "The Dead Wingman"

I hadn't recognized the power of Whitman's "Out of the Cradle Endlessly Rocking" until I happened to read it aloud to a class of young poets; we were all staggered. And not, as so often, by the philosophical breadth of his Inclusiveness–ideas he had developed to quiet a sense of exclusion as a homosexual. Here, following the loss of someone he loved, those ideas clearly failed to provide comfort. Instead, at the beginning, we hear an embodied rhythm, linked with the sea as the mother, the source of life:

> Out of the cradle endlessly rocking,
> Out of the mockingbird's throat, the musical shuttle,
> Out of the Ninth-month midnight...etc.

Then, though the body of the poem is given over to tearing expressions of grief and loss, carried by different musical effects, that initial rhythm unexpectedly reappears in the final lines, promising rejoinder in death with the All.

> The word of the sweetest song and all songs,
> That strong and delicious word which, creeping to my feet,
> (Or like some old crone rocking the cradle, swathed in sweet garments,
> bending aside,)
> The sea whispered me.

The resurgence of that rhythm is one of the most magical effects in poetry.

Henri Coulette's cycle of poems, "The War of the Secret Agents," based on actual events in World War II, consists of monologues by British secret agents sent into occupied France, then captured and, most of them, executed. The cycle's theme, that despite their faults and obvious ineptitude (the British deliberately betrayed them, so hiding other, craftier spies), we must, and do, identify with them as individuals. Such a technique of shorter, individual poems rather than anything of epic lengths and unified meaning, seemed to fit the fragmentation of the modern situation. Lacking any unified field theory for our life's meaning, we must turn to relativisms of some sort—here, identification with the various persons involved in the story. This cycle influenced me toward writing cycles of individual poems, each unified in itself, but only loosely linked within the cycle.

Thomas Hardy's "Afterward" was praised by Robert Lowell as showing 24/20 vision. It *does* have admirable concrete details but I find even more remarkable the way that it conveys the fullness, even the contradictions, of his mind. The surface of the poem carries Hardy's skeptical belief that our only afterlife lies in remembrance by some few neighbors. Yet, the underside of the poem—those same concrete details—is saturated by intimations, and expectations, of resurrection and rebirth. Thus we recognize the fullness of a mind where (as so often) intellection and emotion are poised in conflict; we get a rounded human, not a cardboard cutout erected to support some belief or disbelief.

Ezra Pound's tiny poem,

In a Station of the Metro

The apparition of these faces in the crowd;
    Petals on a wet, black bough.

achieves a surprising expansiveness by its oppositions: the discovery of an image, beautiful and fresh, where we expected dirt, clutter and crowding. Sarah Cleghorn (a nearly forgotten Socialist poet) creates a reversed, but equally surprising opposition through a *double-entendre*:

The Golf Links

The golf links lie so near the mill
    That almost every day
The laboring children can look out
    And see the men at play.

The word "mill" may suggest an idyllic rural scene with a waterwheel; that's transformed to a factory sweatshop where poor children watch the wealthy sporting in their artificial landscape. Last, I'd note a poem by Ruth Soter (who died before her work could receive general notice):

Haiku

Let me look at you,

Invulnerable woman,
When you have a son.

Unlike Japanese haiku, which gain breadth by building networks of ambiguity and reference, this American haiku switches focus and meaning line by line, finally discovering that invulnerability may not be so admirable – if you dare really love someone, you can be hurt.

Randall Jarrell's "The Truth" moves me so deeply that I can't read it aloud without breaking up; so do others, like "The Dead Wingman." Jarrell, one of my teachers, often said that critics were right to rule out sentimentality, but that mustn't be confused with sentiment. His influence pushed me to decide that my poems should deal directly with powerful emotions, with passions.

JULIANA SPAHR

Allen Ginsberg, *Howl*
Gertrude Stein, *Tender Buttons*
Theresa Hak Kyung Cha, *Dictee*
Lyn Hejinian, *My Life*
Kamau Brathwaite, *Middle Passages*
Bruce Andrews, *Give 'Em Enough Rope*
Susan Howe, *My Emily Dickinson*
Cecilia Vicuña, *Unraveling Words and the Weaving of Water*
Harryette Mullen, *Muse & Drudge*

Oh jeez. This is so endless. And changes from day to day. I just did this exercise with my class here where I gave them that chart that Duncan originally made but is published at the back of Spicer's *Collected Books*. And then had them chart their influences. And I made myself do it, just to see how long it would take and also how possible it was and what I would learn. And I ended up with a chart that began with Allen Ginsberg's *Howl* and the *New American* poets. It was *Howl*, in particular, that changed my life–*Howl* and the Sex Pistols, and I found them in what feels like it must have been the same week. Stein is also in there early on. Then an undergraduate degree that immersed me in high modernism although I never lost my suspicions about Pound and Eliot and Yeats. I always answer "Stein" to the question "Stein or Pound?"

Then the chart moved to language poetry and the poetries adjacent to it. I think I answered a version of this question when I wrote *Everybody's Autonomy*. And I answered then Stein, Andrews, Hejinian, Mullen, and Cha. But if I hadn't had Susan Howe and Charles Bernstein as teachers I wouldn't have been able to answer that way (and I might have included them also). Then from there I moved to something that might be closer to a cultural poetics, as in the work of Cecilia Vicuña and Kamau Brathwaite and also in Hawai'i's many poetries and its debates about appropriation, the politics of language, and the responsibilities of literature. This is where I think now. But I've left out along the way all the peer to peer poetry friendships that I owe a huge debt of theft...Catalina Cariaga, Thalia Field, Peter Gizzi, Renee Gladman, Lisa Jarnot, Pamela Lu, Bill Luoma, Jena Osman, Kristen Prevallet, Bhanu Kapil Rider, Susan Schultz, Ida Yoshinaga (this list is endless, so I'll stop now)...And I've left off Myung Mi Kim's *Commons* and Barrett Watten's *Bad History*, two books that I am still under the influence of daily. And I've left off...

ELIZABETH SPIRES

Josephine Jacobsen, *In the Crevice of Time*
A. R. Ammons, *Selected Poems*
A. R. Ammons, *Garbage*
A. R. Ammons, *Tape for the Turn of the Year*
John Berryman, *Homage to Mistress Bradstreet*
Elizabeth Coatsworth, *The Cat Who Went to Heaven*
May Swenson, *In Other Words* (and other individual titles)
William Meredith, *Partial Accounts*
William Meredith, *The Cheer*
William Meredith, *Hazard, the Painter*
Gwen Harwood (individual titles)

These are authors and books that I greatly admire, and that I have been influenced by, but that seem to me "overlooked."

DAVID ST. JOHN

Percy Bysshe Shelley, *Selected Poems*
Stéphane Mallarmé, *The Complete Poems*
William Butler Yeats, *Collected Poems*
Wallace Stevens, *Collected Poems*
D. H. Lawrence, *Look! We Have Come Through!!*
D. H. Lawrence, *Birds, Beasts, and Flowers*
Elizabeth Bishop, *The Complete Poems*
Paul Eluard, *Selected Writings*
Federico García Lorca, *Selected Verse*
Rainer Maria Rilke, *The Duino Elegies*

From the sheer diaphanous beauty of poets like Shelley, Mallarmé, and Stevens, a beauty laced with profound intellectual rigor and meditative nuance, to the Whitmanic passions of Lawrence and the welding of mystery with formal acuity in Yeats, I can trace a gathering brilliance that I feel in poetry as it writhes its way out of the Nineteenth and into the Twentieth Century. Certainly, the lyric ease and precision of observation, so famous in Bishop, both remind us of the necessity of such human grace–and of a complex clarity–in great poetry. Eluard's poems of love reveal a world honeycombed with sexuality and tenderness; Lorca's poetry excites both our instincts for ancient ballad and song as well as allowing us a new, raw vision of the modern world. Rilke grows more troubling to us by the day, doesn't he? His great work touches the terror of otherness, of death, while–like Lawrence–celebrating the elemental realms of the animal and of the child. All of these voices conspire to speak of human compassion and visionary hopes. When we look to the poets who sustain us, this is what we expect.

GERALD STERN

The Book of Amos
Ovid, *Tristia*
William Shakespeare, *King Lear*
Samuel Taylor Coleridge, *Poems*
Hart Crane, *The Collected Poems*

Amos is the fiercest and one of the earliest of the Hebrew prophets. His message of justice is clear and simple.

Tristia is the mature voice of a lost, bewildered, self-pitying, almost-modern, touching Roman poet. His exile pre-dates and anticipates the modern exile in many ways.

King Lear is the most beautiful, unbearable human character in literature. He stands alongside Job and Gilgamesh.

Coleridge, for me, even more than Wordsworth, is the most human, personal, suffering poet of the last two centuries, especially "Frost at Midnight" and the "Ode to Dejection." I read him as if he were next door.

I have been a life long admirer of Crane's poetry. He, even more than Stevens, retains the original power and mystery. His language is always shockingly fresh. It is that language I adore.

VIRGIL SUÁREZ

Federico García Lorca
Edgar Allen Poe
Pablo Neruda
Denise Levertov
James Dickey
Li Po
Adrian C. Louis
José Martí
Sylvia Plath
Gwendolyn Brooks

Federico García Lorca (everything of his, including plays) was a big influence on my work because of the rhythms and the simplicity of language. Lorca is a master of the short line, of repetition. Repetition to build effect of sound. I have been reading him (and revisiting his work with my students) all of my life. I think some of the best poetry of his is also to be found in his plays, the masterpieces like *Yerma* and *The House of Bernarda Alba*. Also, there's a pastoral, lyrical tonality to the work that thrills me.

Edgar Allen Poe was the first American poet I read while still in junior high school. I fell in love with the mesmeric quality of the work. The sound and meter. The fact that Poe, through his work, takes you to another place. Imagined, invented, whatever you want to call it, but he takes you to this other place and you are more than willing to follow. It's the gothic allure of his enchanting language. Also that when you are still young enough to really appreciate pure morbidity. I still love him and his great poems.

Where would most poets be without the liberation and influence of Pablo Neruda's infamous *Odes*? Like Whitman, he is the other wholly American (not only our hemisphere) vernacular poet. His *Twenty Love Poems & a Song of Despair* can still be thrilling and exciting. Nobody can rival Neruda's gargantuan appetite for beauty and truth, and influence.

Denise Levertov is wonderful with her lyricism and her images. I still return to her wonderful collection *O Taste & See*. I read her work for the electricity of line, enjambment, and exactness of diction. She's a master of subtlety.

I read Mr. Dickey with great pleasure still because I've never fully recovered from his lines, his diction, his ability to juggle and create zingers–those word combos that are thrilling and at the same time take you out of your skin. The first poem I read of his which marked me forever was "Adultery." It's amazing what he can do with language and image.

Regarding Li Po, three words come to mind: simplicity, energy, evocative. I learned that a poet can meander, can look at the simple things in life and build poetry out of it. Friendship, wine, rivers, the moon. The things that still matter to humans.

Adrian C. Louis: No other contemporary poet is so possessed with what Lorca called "duende." Mr. Louis' voice is remarkable, memorable. His poetry is pure fire, and I can't help but relish its burning. No other poet has this kind of honest, amazing testament to a life lived on the margins. A life recorded in gorgeous struggle to survive, to live on, and to work against all odds. Mr. Louis has written a lasting record of the genocide inflicted upon Native Americans in this country.

José Martí is the patriot poet of Cuba. I grew up listening to my grandmother and, later, my mother recite him to me when I bathed as a child. When they put me to bed. In the Caribbean and Latin America one learns to be a politically minded poet through reading José Martí. His work and life awakens a great spirit of human consciousness in everyone who reads him. Martí claimed that everyone must write a book, have a child, and plant a tree. Not necessarily in that order.

I read Sylvia Plath for the images. The tough life. The fact that she worked with meter, sound, rhyme. Left a legacy of pain and a reminder to all young poets not to take her own personal life as a marker. Don't kill yourself over your art.

Gwendolyn Brooks is a poet of grace, of amazing spirit. I love Ms. Brooks' poems for the world they reveal, reaffirm. The fact that she wrote better than any other poet about what it feels like to be an outsider. Not to belong, and still survive.

DAVID TRINIDAD

Joe Brainard, *I Remember*
Dennis Cooper, *The Tenderness of the Wolves*
Tim Dlugos, *Entre Nous*
Edward Field, *Variety Photoplays*
Alice Notley, *Waltzing Matilda*
Frank O'Hara, *Lunch Poems*
Sylvia Plath, *Ariel*
Sappho, trans. Mary Barnard
James Schuyler, *The Morning of the Poem*
Anne Sexton, *Love Poems*

The books that meant the most to me when I was in college (early-mid 1970's) were the Sexton (I discovered *Love Poems* while browsing through the poetry section of a bookstore in a Los Angeles shopping mall), the Plath (assigned in a lit class), the O'Hara (a strange roommate gave me *Lunch Poems* for my twentieth birthday, with an equally strange note: "You—in 15 years?"), and the Field (the "Old Movies" section of *Variety Photoplays* pointed toward new and exciting possibilities for me). Later, through my friends Dennis Cooper and Tim Dlugos (whose work had a BIG impact on me), I discovered such New York School gems as Joe Brainard's *I Remember*, James Schuyler's *The Morning of the Poem*, and Alice Notley's *Waltzing Matilda*—all wonderful, magical books. I don't remember when I discovered the Sappho, but nothing has ever beat it for clarity, brevity, and beauty.

PAUL VIOLI

The Troubadours
Romans: Virgil, Horace, Catullus, Ovid, etc.
Wordsworth and Coleridge's Conversation Poems
Walt Whitman, "Out of the Cradle Endlessly Rocking"
Keats, Byron (*Don Juan*) and Shelley ("Ode to the West Wind")
Ezra Pound, *The Pisan Cantos*, viz. LXXXI
William Carlos Williams, "Asphodel, That Greeny Flower"
The first 3/4 of *The Random House Book of Twentieth-Century French
    Poetry*
Dante
William Shakespeare

What books have been essential to me? (Mine!) An impossible and irresistible question. I can manage better if I take broad and narrow strokes–books and specific works, a mostly traditional list of radically inventive poems.

My answer would be somewhat different if you asked me next week. Omit Chaucer, Villon, Marvell, The Tribe of Ben, Yeats, Fitzgerald, Rilke, Mayakovsky, a slew of Japanese and Chinese anthologies? Lewis Carroll! I'm changing the list already. I'll take "essential" to mean poems that I love more than others, though the latter, which includes a lot of contemporary work, remains influential and inspirational but not as crucial when compared to those that I have returned to continually over the decades: poems that even in translation leave me awe-struck.

KAREN VOLKMAN

Rainer Maria Rilke, *Sonnets to Orpheus*
Thomas Traherne, *Centuries of Meditation*
George Herbert, *The Temple*
Hans Christian Andersen, *The Snow Queen*
Emily Dickinson, *Collected Poems*
Sylvia Plath, *Ariel*
Simone Weil, *Gravity and Grace*

The 55 *Sonnets to Orpheus* were written in less than three weeks when Rilke was deeply engaged in *The Duino Elegies*. He later referred to "the little rust-colored sail" of the sonnets as counterpoint to the *Elegies'* larger expansive movements. There is a delicacy of tone and a strangeness to these poems that has fascinated me for years, first in English translation (my preference is M. D. Herder Norton's) and for the last few years in German (it was learning German and re-encountering the works as formal sonnets that partly led to my current work in the form). Rilke's fascination with other states of being–a flower, a mirror, a dog, a stone fountain–here assumes a tone both reverential and vulnerable, even humble. As Orphic translator, he communicates in song-ciphers that sound far beyond their medium.

***

Traherne's *Centuries of Meditation* is a work of theology. Written in books of 100 numbered passages, the *Centuries* are part prose poem, part spiritual autobiography, part ecstatic witness. Addressed to a close friend, the meditations are charged with an intimacy and sweetness that make their revelations deeply personal and in some sense a secular sharing.

***

George Herbert's *The Temple* is an architecture of reverence through a range of forms and tones.

***

The Snow Queen begins with malicious demons carrying a diabolical distorting mirror joyously through the skies, till it shatters and rains malign shards into the eyes of humans. One of the first stories I remember reading as a child, and one I go back to for its strangeness and intensity of image: little Gerda throwing her red shoes to the waves, which send them bobbing back to her, the Little Robber Maiden tickling her pet reindeer's neck with a knife, the Flowers' dreams, the austere palace of ice. Like other of Andersen's tales, *The Snow Queen* fuses brutality and innocence in a landscape of inevitability and frightening swerves of fate.

***

Dickinson ("I leaned upon the Awe–") has of course been essential to any number of writers, female poets in particular, for her obliquity, astonishing intelligence, and uncompromising style. She revealed to me a mode of dealing with the abstract as a palpable presence in our lives, and a way of lending contour to that elusive dimension of experience.

***

Like Dickinson, Plath has greatly influenced me in her wrestling with abstraction, particularly with states of terror that challenge the limits of articulation: "Let the stars / Plummet to their dark address, / Let the mercuric / Atoms that cripple drip / Into the terrible well."

***

Simone Weil is another uncompromising intelligence wrestling with faith, doubt, and terror. Her concision and aphoristic urgency in this posthumous collection (culled from her journal writings) revealed to me how a spareness and precision could resonate with a force far exceeding its apparent means, charging the space around it (either blank or the implicit space between disjunctive moments) with a wealth of energy and urge: "The 'I' leaves its mark on the world as it destroys."

DAVID WAGONER

〰️

Joseph Campbell, *The Hero with a Thousand Faces*
W. H. Auden, *Collected Poems*
Wallace Stevens, *Harmonium*
William Butler Yeats, *The Collected Poems*
Mitford M. Mathews, *A Dictionary of Americanisms*
Mark Twain, *The Collected Works*
Joseph Conrad, *Heart of Darkness*
Graham Greene
Henry David Thoreau, *Journal*

Campbell's *The Hero with a Thousand Faces* felt like a genuine revelation to me in my early twenties. I recognized in its persuasive outline of the hero's journey the unconscious pattern followed by a great many narratives I had admired–*The Red Badge of Courage*, *Heart of Darkness*, *Catcher in the Rye*, etc.–and felt I had a new insight into my own plot-making.

Auden's versatility, especially in the early poems, gave me a broadened sense of what a poem could be and how I could approach the writing of a poem from a choice of many directions.

I was amazed by Wallace Stevens' wonderful ear and his surprising diction.

With Yeats, I was particularly struck by his ability to reproduce the speaking voice, and not just his own, on the page and to dramatize it.

Mathews' *A Dictionary of Americanisms* is an absorbing collection of new words (or new usages of old words) and phrases that originated in the United States, supported by quotations from letters, journals, novels, poems, newspapers, speeches, etc. from Colonial times to the 1940's. It shows clearly the organic growth of American speech with all its strengths and potential weaknesses.

If you skip the pomposities of Twain, don't skip any of the vernacular, include the after-dinner speeches, and put special emphasis on *Life on the Mississippi* and *Roughing It*, you may feel as refreshed by his handling of our language as I have since grade school.

I was deeply intrigued by the unusual structure of Conrad's *Heart of Darkness*, its slowly building power, and the way it haunted me afterward. Not one unnecessary sentence.

Read the novels of Graham Greene, especially *The Power and the Glory* and the early "Entertainments," particularly *The Confidential Agent*, *The Ministry of Fear*, and *Brighton Rock*. One reviewer of my first novel, *The Man in the Middle*, said "It gives off heavy Graham Greenish fumes," and he was right.

I discovered *Journal* very late, but it convinced me that Thoreau did his best work when he wasn't yet writing for the public and that he could have been the best American poet of the 19th Century, with the exception of Emily Dickinson, if he hadn't been so self-consciously crippled by the conventions of his time.

CHARLES HARPER WEBB

Dylan Thomas, *Collected Poems*
Sylvia Plath, *Ariel*
Edward Field, *Stand Up Friend, With Me*
James Tate, *The Oblivion Ha-Ha*
Philip Levine, *They Feed They Lion*
Russell Edson, *The Intuitive Journey & Other Works*
Ron Koertge, *Diary Cows*
Edward Hirsch, *Wild Gratitude*

Rather than cite classic authors that every poet should have read, I've chosen to list books which had a major impact on my development as a poet when I was struggling to define myself as one. If these books are out of print, other books by the authors will likely do as well. They are listed, not in order of importance, but in the order in which I discovered them.

Dylan Thomas can be heavy sledding, and can exert a bad influence on developing poets; still, at his best, he shows as well as any poet of the 20th century what the lyric poem can do. Reading "Fern Hill" aloud, I still risk bursting into tears.

Sylvia Plath's *Ariel*: Intensity, energy, audacity, passion, brilliant metaphors, and just plain madness. What can I say?

Field showed me how moving plain-spoken truth-telling can be, when coupled with an idiosyncratic imagination, and genuine vulnerability. "The Bride of Frankenstein" helped me to see pop culture (and in fact the whole world) as potential poetry. "Graffiti" is "Fern Hill" set in New York, with dirty words.

Tate is fantastic for jolting the mind off its usual track, and for the permission he gives fellow writers to play. The energy, imagination, and wacky fun that crackles in his poems has inspired me since I discovered him back in the seventies.

Philip Levine showed me a way to write seriously without becoming ponderous. His work expresses deep anger and deep tenderness from a profoundly male perspective. His work, in short, has *cojones*. He does wonderful things with (relatively) plain speech, and those mainstays of fiction: character and narrative.

Reading Russell Edson was, for me, an all-out epiphany. I'd been having thoughts (and dreams) like his little poem-stories ever since I was a child, but hadn't had a clue what to do with them. Edson is mind-expanding without the dead brain cells and trips to the ER.

I first encountered Koertge's work when he submitted it to *Madrona*, a magazine I was helping to edit. As a recent graduate of a Very Serious Writing Program, I wasn't sure if Koertge was a brilliant comic and irreverent provocateur, or if he'd completely miscalculated the effects of his work. In either case, the poems were what no one from my program would have dared to be: hilarious. Koertge proved to be a wonderful corrective to the pompous, serious-as-a-bladder-infection stuff that the prestige places were full of. And he still is today.

I discovered Hirsch at a time when I was trying to break out of a cavernous rut and remake myself as a poet. The tenderness, accessibility, humanity, willingness to take emotional risks, and non-stodgy seriousness of Hirsch's poems opened possibilities for me to add depth and resonance to my own work, without sacrificing the spirit that made it tick.

DARA WIER

Your invitation is kindly received; your assignment impossible. Having repeatedly tried to shorten a list more upwards into the 100s, it seems one conclusion is that just about everything seems essential. But that will get us nowhere, so arbitrarily here goes two vastly different lists:

Readings in child-like adventures:

The Brothers Grimm
The Old Testament
The Stories of Edgar Allen Poe
The Golden Treasury of Natural History
My Poetry Book: An Anthology of Modern Verse for Boys and Girls
Voyages in English
Mark Twain, *Tom Sawyer*
Mark Twain, *Huckleberry Finn*
Michael Faraday, *The Chemical History of a Candle*

The Brothers Grimm lent credence to complications surrounding my surroundings' surroundings.

The Old Testament underscored chaos, retribution, tenacity in high falutin syntax and vocabulary and developed its story in both completely inevitable and surprising twists and turns and shortcuts and fullstops and reconsiderations.

The Stories of Edgar Allan Poe provided my first inkling of reasoning's rapacity.

The Golden Treasury of Natural History, for situating me in the universe.

I'm including something called *My Poetry Book: An Anthology of Modern Verse for Boys and Girls*, given to me when I turned eleven. While reading some of the included poems entertained me, what I returned to over and over again was how the poems looked on a page. I liked looking at the arrangements of lines just as I was compelled to watch boats' wakes approaching the riverbank or field rows unfurling.

An elementary text entitled *Voyages in English* was an amusing way of learning all about grammar and the elements of composition useful to imagining the endless possible ways of building sentences, etc. *Voyages* was a catholic text written to indoctrinate young readers and writers, so it was also instructive regarding issues of "audience," how not to condescend to a reader, how not to be preachy, or worse, didactic, how not to pretend you don't know what you are doing, and so on.

With my locale being situated at the mouth of the Mississippi, naturally I was inclined to think of Tom Sawyer and Huckleberry Finn as family. Twain's conspiratorial reader/writer tone was very satisfying.

I include Michael Faraday's *The Chemical History of a Candle* for its absorbing, precise and obsessive philosophical analysis of everything regarding a candle; by being fascinated with this book the idea of what abstraction might be slowly began to dawn on me.

Books that came later:

Franz Kafka, *The Complete Stories*
Wallace Stevens, *The Collected Poems*
Hart Crane, *The Bridge*
William Carlos Williams, *The Embodiment of Knowledge*
Witold Gombrowicz, *Cosmos*
Emily Dickinson, *The Complete Letters*
Christopher Smart, *Jubilate Agno*
Vasko Popa's poems in translation
John Clare's poems and prose
John Ashbery, *Flow Chart*

Here is where being brief is unbearably (leaving out so much that's been certainly essential) constricting. This list should contain so many it would take several weeks to complete it responsibly and truly, so I'll leave it at that for now, without comment.

RICHARD WILBUR

John Milton, *Paradise Lost*
Robert Frost, *Collected Poems*
Philip Larkin, *Collected Poems*
Homer, *The Odyssey*
Timothy Steele, *Missing Measures*
John Hollander, *Rhyme's Reason*
Thomas Carper and Derek Attridge, *Meter and Meaning*
Lewis Turco, *The New Book of Forms*
Edward Lear, *The Nonsense Book*
Peter Taylor, *A Summons to Memphis*

I think it is good for young poets to have heartbreaking ambitions, and so I recommend Milton, who can make one wish for the power and mastery to speak not merely for oneself but for a culture, as *The Odyssey* also speaks for a culture. Timothy Steele's book, which considers poetic form from ancient times until the present, will be useful to anyone who still confuses free verse with progress and daring. No one who has the knack of writing poetry ever needs to scan a line or analyze the function of a stanza, but I mention several books which provide a lively vocabulary for speaking of form and of our wondrous heritage of forms. I suggest Edward Lear, as I might have suggested Lewis Carroll or Gavin Ewart, because poetry at every level is full of play and pleasure, or had better be. Peter Taylor's narrative prose is full of nuance, and the wording of poetry should not be less subtle than such splendid prose.

C. K. WILLIAMS

W. H. Auden, *Collected Poems*
Charles Baudelaire, *Les Fleurs du Mal*
Elizabeth Bishop, *Complete Poems*
William Blake, *The Marriage of Heaven and Hell*
William Blake, *Songs of Innocence and Songs of Experience*
Emily Dickinson, *Poems*
T. S. Eliot, *The Four Quartets*
Robert Frost, *Collected Poems*
George Herbert, *Poems*
Gerard Manley Hopkins, *Poems*
John Keats, *Poems* (particularly the odes)
Robert Lowell, *Life Studies*
Robert Lowell, *For the Union Dead*
John Milton, *Paradise Lost* and "Lycidas"
Rainer Maria Rilke, *The Duino Elegies*
Rainer Maria Rilke, *New Poems*
William Carlos Williams, *Pictures from Bruegel*
Walt Whitman, "Song of Myself"
William Butler Yeats, *The Tower*

I find it impossible to limit my list of "Essential Titles" to five or ten; in fact, if I hadn't decided to limit my list to poets who are no longer alive, it would be still longer. All the works that are here have been very frequently–for some of them more or less non-stop–on my desk since I began to write poems. The thought comes to me that they're the books that not only taught me how to write, but saved my life. I don't quite know what I mean by that, perhaps that they made my life more than saved it, but I'll leave it like that.

C. D. Wright

BOOKS TO LIVE WITH

Walt Whitman, *Leaves of Grass*
Emily Dickinson, *Collected Poetry*
Thomas Hardy, *Selected Poetry*
Gerard Manley Hopkins, *Selected Poetry*
Gertrude Stein, *Selected Writings*
Ezra Pound, *The Cantos*

Lorine Niedecker, *Collected Works*
William Bronk, *Life Supports*
William Bronk, *Selected Poems*
Frank O'Hara, *Selected Poems*
Robert Creeley, *Selected Poems*
W. S. Merwin, *The Second Four Books of Poems*
W. S. Merwin, *The Folding Cliffs: A Narrative*
John Ashbery, *Flow Chart*

John Taggart, *Standing Wave*
Michael Ondaatje, *The Collected Works of Billy the Kid*
Sharon Doubiago, *Hard Country*
Ron Silliman, *Tjanting*
Mei Mei Berssenbrugge, *Empathy*
Frank Stanford, *The Battlefield Where the Moon Says I Love You*
Carolyn Forché, *The Angel of History*
Arthur Sze, *The Red-Shifting Web*
Theresa Hak Kyung Cha, *Dictee*
Forrest Gander, *Torn Awake*

5 in translation:

Cesare Pavese, *Hard Labor*
Jean Follain, *Transparence of the World*
Jacques Roubaud, *Some Thing Black*
Inger Christensen, *Alphabet*
Jaime Saenz, *Immanent Visitor: Selected Poems*

Poets' autobiographies:

Keith Waldrop, *Light While There is Light: An American History*
Louise Bogan, *Journey Around My Room*
Michael Ondaatje, *Running in the Family*
Lyn Hejinian, *My Life*

For writers no longer living, I named either a selected or a major collection (for ready availability). I know individual titles are preferable, but the important thing is to get the word in hand.

These lists are very difficult. For one, I am fickle about some books and loyal to others in spite of my judgment of them having modified, and for another, I sometimes am reluctant to share, even with my students with whom I share anyway, of course. And then, if they don't like them, I am stricken. Poetry is the ultimately tailored medium. I never really liked anyone else picking out my underthings.

The nineteenth-century born poets who have stuck to me most are:

Whitman, Dickinson, Hardy, Hopkins, Stein, and Pound. I'm not an Eliot woman though I read him under the direction of the same professor, Ben Kimpel, who so brilliantly guided his class through *The Cantos*. That particular tome probably gave me a head for wildly inclusive works.

Of poets born in the first quarter of the twentieth century or thereabouts, I favor:

Niedecker, Bronk, O'Hara, Creeley, Merwin, and Ashbery. I came to Ashbery last, and Merwin first. Merwin was probably my first encounter with a late lyric. I was and am haunted by Merwin.
I like Niedecker for her condensery. How does she do it?
I like Bronk for the Stevens-minus-the-gewgaw. He terrifies me.
I like Creeley for his primecoat address. Spirit/mind wholeness and openness. O rare.
I read O'Hara for a pick-me-up although I am well aware of the undertow.
I read Ashbery for his volubility. Logocopia.
They are all, virtuosos. They have all written poems and books of poems that have changed the genre. "Made it new." They are all essential.

Among peers it is harder to make a determination. Rather it is harder to sort the why you like and the why you don't like. I chose individual titles here. There are many more I would name. But these titles among the many made their indelible mark on me and my psyche:

Mei Mei Berssenbrugge: *Empathy*

It presents a finely worked, nearly impenetrable surface, an aestheticized world view.

Theresa Hak Kyung Cha: *Dictee*

It's that Walter Benjamin thing, all great works either found a genre or dissolve one. I don't know how great it is or is not, but it is definitely a genre-buster.

Sharon Doubiago: *Hard Country*

It was the first epic of its kind, the first map of the New World I had ever read.

Carolyn Forché: *The Angel of History*

No one has stronger descriptive powers. And is so pressing in her accounting. No one else has given herself the charge for this accounting in quite such mesmerizing terms.

Forrest Gander: *Torn Awake*

Being privy—to some of their circumstances yet not to others—has not disturbed the moving mystery of words and the marvels they carry within themselves that these poems invariably provoke in me.

Michael Ondaatje: *The Collected Works of Billy the Kid*

This book gives such unstinting pleasure. The language, the composition is so ingenious, so right.

Ron Silliman: *Tjanting*

This is full of acts I wasn't used to seeing a sentence committing.

Frank Stanford: *The Battlefield Where the Moon Says I Love You*

I went down this river, and all but drowned in it. Since Faulkner, there hasn't been a writer from the South who could touch him.

Arthur Sze: *The Red Shifting Web*

A rapturous poetry, and one of transformation, that causes the words to shine through their factual darkness.

John Taggart: *Standing Wave*

Gertrude Stein tapped most securely into the joy of repetition, but Taggart found the fold in the language, and that opens the ear to hitherto ignored aural satisfaction.

CHARLES WRIGHT

St. Augustine, *The Confessions*
Dante, *The Divine Comedy*
Ezra Pound, *Selected Poems*
Ezra Pound, *The Cantos*
Eugenio Montale, *La Bufera e altro*
Emily Dickinson, *Collected Poems*
Ernest Hemingway, *Collected Stories*
Gerard Manley Hopkins, *Collected Poems*
William Carlos Williams, *Pictures from Bruegel*
Donald Justice, *The Summer Anniversaries*
The King James Bible

  I don't know what to say about these books—some were "essential" technically (Justice, Pound, Hemingway), others in a more hidden and intimately profound way (St. Augustine, *Bible*, Dickinson). In which ever way, I was putty in their hands in their given time. Or Play Dough at the least. One could probably add others, but, as Pound says (quoting someone else—Jefferson?), "Tempus loquendi, tempus tacendi."

FRANZ WRIGHT

Heraclitus, *The Presocratics*, ed. Philip Wheelwright
The Fourth Gospel (*The New Oxford Annotated Bible*)
Arthur Rimbaud
René Char, *Leaves of Hypnos*, trans. Cid Corman
John Donne
William Blake, *Songs of Innocence and Songs of Experience*
Theodore Roethke
Paul Celan
Osip Mandelstam
Tu Fu, trans. Kenneth Rexroth
Rainer Maria Rilke
Franz Kafka, "At Night"
Emily Dickinson
Hart Crane

It is very difficult to limit the list to 10 texts, but this is what comes to mind on this particular day.

"What we see when asleep is dream; when awake, death." This quotation is drawn from the fragments of the major Greek Presocratic, Heraclitus. My favorite version of him may be found in *The Presocratics*, edited by Philip Wheelwright. I find a never ending source of energy in him because his words (like everything I consider to be authentic in writing) appear to emanate from a part of the mind to which the distinction between art, religion, poetry, and prayer has not occurred.

To me, the Fourth Gospel (in its entirety) is the single greatest poem of any time or language. With stunning and heartbreaking beauty, the author employs symbols from common experience–such as bread, water, light, wine, life, shepherd, door–and contrasting universal and timeless images such as light/darkness, truth/lies, love/hatred, death/resurrection, to make his meaning utterly clear and gripping to any reader regardless of background or literacy. Its central message is God's shocking revelation to human beings in John 15:14: "You are my friends."

The complete poems and "prose" of Arthur Rimbaud who, aside from being the only poet to create major and immortal works during childhood, provides unfortunate proof that one does not need to be a particularly good human being to be an extraordinarily great and moving artist. And one must not forget to mention his master, Baudelaire.

Leaves of Hypnos, the secret wartime journal kept by René Char during his service in the French Resistance fighting the Nazi occupiers in the woods and fields of France, in its excellent 1973 Mushinsha/Grossman translation by Cid Corman. The only Rimbaud-influenced poet to genuinely extend (and hugely humanize) the achievement of that strange child, Char began his career among the Surrealists and almost immediately outgrew them. (The radiantly aphoristic technique at the heart of his inspirations leads back to his beloved Heraclitus, by the way.) This holy book concludes with the following:

The Rose of the Oak

> Each of the letters that compose your name, O Beauty, on the honor roll of sufferings, espouses the level simplicity of the sun, is inscribed in the giant phrase that bars the sky, and is associated with man bent upon confusing his destiny with its indomitable opposite: hope.

What follows is just one of many passages from John Donne which I can barely bring myself to read:

> Since she must go, and I must mourn, come night,
> Environ me with darkness, whilst I write:
> Shadow that hell unto me, which alone
> I am to suffer when my love is gone.

The authenticity in these lines is bound to be instantly shattering to any person who is not a psychopath. As a technician, Donne is as great as Shakespeare.

It is no secret that William Blake was a somewhat odd guy, but he is also the author of "London," which I consider to be the single greatest lyric poem in the English language.

Theodore Roethke is, in my opinion, the single greatest poet the United States has produced. The following passage (from "The Lost Son") is far from being his most magnificent, but it is one of my favorites:

> It was beginning winter,
> An in-between time,
> The landscape still partly brown:
> The bones of weeds kept swinging in the wind,
> Above the blue snow.
>
> It was beginning winter,
> The light moved slowly over the frozen field,

Over the dry seed-crowns,
The beautiful surviving bones
Swinging in the wind.

Light traveled over the wide field;
Stayed.
The weeds stopped swinging.
The mind moved, not alone.
Through the clear air, in the silence.

Was it light?
Was it light within?
Was it light within light?
Stillness becoming alive,
Yet still?

A lively understandable spirit
Once entertained you. It will come again.
Be still.
Wait.

Paul Celan seems to me the greatest European poet of the twentieth century. (Along with Osip Mandelstam, T. S. Eliot, Elizabeth Bishop, Yeats, Hart Crane, Stevens, Montale, Johannes Bobrowski, Gunther Eich, Louise Glück, Jean Valentine, Fanny Howe–one could go on, it was quite a century.) Read every blessed word of Paul Celan.

And read every word of Osip Mandelstam.

And every word of Tu Fu.

I spent twenty years of my life trying to figure out how to render a handful of Rainer Maria Rilke's poems into English. In recent decades, with some notable exceptions (Young, Bly, Kinnell, and, frankly, me) Rilke has been talked, and poorly translated, to death. But nothing, not even some well known radical feminist sour-pusses, can diminish the accomplishment which, again, makes the prayer/poem distinction all nonsense. If you have not read him, especially the great middle period of *Neue Gedichte*, please do. If you have, reread him. No one like him in the world.

In Kafka's short prose piece "At Night" there is a dimension, a dark tolling musical dimension, to the prose which only-English readers sadly miss out on, but the old Tania and James Stern translation of this particular small masterpiece (a redundant term, since this painfully skeptical, hilarious and profoundly devout man wrote nothing that was not a masterpiece), composed during a few stolen hours at his beloved sister's apartment where he went to escape family hubbub, still conveys some of the original's shattering poignancy.

At Night

> Deeply lost in the night. Just as one sometimes lowers one's head to reflect, thus to be utterly lost in the night. All around people are asleep. It's just play acting, an innocent self-deception, that they sleep in houses, in safe beds, under a safe roof, stretched out or curled up on mattresses, in sheets, under blankets; in reality they have flocked together as they had once upon a time and again later in a deserted region, a camp in the open, a countless number of men, an army, a people, under a cold sky on cold earth, collapsed where once they had stood, forehead pressed on the arm, face to the ground, breathing quietly. And you are watching, are one of the watchmen, you find the next one by brandishing a burning stick from the brushwood pile beside you. Why are you watching? Someone must watch, it is said. Someone must be there.

Auden wrote somewhere that Kafka bears the same relationship to our age that Dante and Shakespeare bore to theirs. And while this is certainly the case, it might also be added that he accomplished far more than mir-roring or personifying in his words the faithless and mechanical horror of the twentieth century–he was actually a prophesier. He was unable to realize his dream of a new life in Palestine and died an early painful death in 1924 (a couple years before the death of Rilke, a great admirer of his), and thus was spared the fate of his sister, who was murdered not that many years later at Auschwitz.

Emily Dickinson is the secret saint of all poets (as perhaps van Gogh is of all painters). Again, read every spiritual and adorably earth-ly word.

If I am to be able to go on sleeping at night, it is important to include the name Hart Crane (who is, incidentally, one of the most radiant minds ever to be damaged, darkened, and finally extinguished by the disease of alcoholism), that uncatagorizable American successor of Rimbaud, Donne, the earlier Elizabethans and, in a very real way, Walt Whitman.

Among Americans, I'd also want to mention Stevens, and then Williams–one name begets another (and it is quite impossible not to wish one could list one hundred texts instead of ten, or rather the fourteen I have now overflowed into). I love Stevens. Who doesn't? But if I had to choose one, my personal allegiance belongs with Hart Crane. To my taste Crane contains, in every word, the authentic, human, real, necessary thing, though I am aware that Stevens is by far the greater poet.

DEAN YOUNG

Ovid, *The Metamorphosis*
Shaking the Pumpkin, ed. Jerome Rothenberg
The Norton Anthology of Poetry, third edit.
The Essential Haiku, ed. Robert Hass
Bert Holldobler and E. O. Wilson, *The Ants*
Dada Painters and Poets, ed. Robert Motherwell
The Random House Book of Twentieth Century French Poetry, ed. Paul
    Auster
Andre Breton, *Manifestos of Surrealism*
Robert Hughes, *Shock of the New*
David Attenborough, *Life of Earth*
Twentieth Century Latin American Poetry, ed. Stephen Tapscott
Oulipo Compendium, eds. Harry Mathews and Alastair Brotche

The Metamorphosis: Lust as a poetic device and vice versa.
After this read Roberto Calasso's *The Marriage of Cadmus and
Harmony* to get the full force of myth's variation.

Shaking the Pumpkin: Instant contact with the deep needs and
necessities of poetry.

The Norton Anthology of Poetry: Or something else where you
can find Frost, Hopkins, Blake, etc. Mostly worthless when it gets to the
later parts of the 20th Century.

The Essential Haiku: Restorative to clutter. The humility and
power of seeing the world. And yet and yet.

The Ants: Anyone who is ever going to work in an English
Department needs to know something about insects, and why not start
with the most noble soldiers of Achilles.

Dada Painters and Poets: Dada, where the great sabotage of art
really kicks in. The restoring and reinvigorating power of the tantrum.

The Random House Book of Twentieth Century French Poetry:
The French pretty much invented twentieth century art. An anthology of
inventors, all second to Apollonaire.

The Manifestos of Surrealism: The most important and influential
aesthetic statement of the twentieth century and if anyone says different,
they've never read it. Or woke up dead.

Shock of the New: Helpful visuals. The excitement of aesthetic
possibility uninhibited by a symbolic medium. I'd rather be a painter.

Life on Earth: Our family history. Why we can still breathe
underwater and fly, why we flash at night and sing with our legs.

Twentieth Century Latin American Poetry: The sword goes through the neck instantly severing the spinal column ole!

Oulipo Compendium: Antidote to above. Things to do on an empty night.

PAUL ZIMMER

William Butler Yeats, *The Collected Poems*
William Shakespeare, *The Collected Plays*
Mark Twain, *Huckleberry Finn*
Henry David Thoreau, *Walden, or Life in the Woods*
Emily Dickinson, *The Collected Poems*
John Clare, *The Collected Poems*
Federico García Lorca, *The Poems*
The Brontës
Thomas Hardy

I know these are quite obvious volumes to cite as influences. There are few surprises here, but these are the books that have remained at the center of my consciousness from the very first time I turned their pages. I return to them again and again. They were my original sources, and they remain so.

I read Yeats for his sonority and his magic. I turn to Shakespeare to realize and imagine what greatness is. I cherish Twain for his unashamed reliance on wit and human character. From my first moments with *Walden*, Thoreau has taught me how to pay attention to, and be respectful of the non-human world. Emily Dickinson has taught me to be spare, and to trust the quick turns of my consciousness. I read John Clare to gain strength–and I marvel at his bravery. Federico García Lorca has taught me to sift and pay attention to my precious dreams. I read and reread the Brontës and Thomas Hardy's novels to remain aware of the importance of *story* in all writing.

THE MOST FREQUENTLY LISTED AUTHORS

Because readers are sure to wonder, below in alphabetical order are the authors whose books (and/or single poems) are listed three or more times. In some cases, all three titles are listed by the same poet. For instance, Elizabeth Spires recommends three books by A. R. Ammons and three by William Meredith, and Alice Friman lists three by Roberto Calasso. On the other hand, the sixteen listings of Walt Whitman come from sixteen poets, and John Ashbery is listed by nine poets, who cite seven books.

A. R. Ammons (3)
John Ashbery (9)
W. H. Auden (4)
Basho (3)
Charles Baudelaire (4)
Elizabeth Bishop (8)
William Blake (6)
William Bronk (3)
Gwendolyn Brooks (3)
Roberto Calasso (3)
Samuel Taylor Coleridge (3)
Hart Crane (7)
Robert Creeley (6)
Dante (5)
Emily Dickinson (16)
John Donne (6)
Fyodor Dostoevsky (5)
T. S. Eliot (6)
Edward Field (6)
Carolyn Forché (3)
Robert Frost (4)
Allen Ginsberg (7)
Louise Glück (5)
Thomas Hardy (3)
Lyn Hejinian (3)
George Herbert (4)
Ernest Hemingway (4)
Homer (4)
Gerard Manley Hopkins (4)
James Joyce (4)
Franz Kafka (3)

John Keats (6)
Galway Kinnell (3)
Federico García Lorca (8)
Robert Lowell (3)
Herman Melville (5)
William Meredith (3)
W. S. Merwin (4)
Harryette Mullen (3)
Pablo Neruda (5)
Lorine Niedecker (4)
Alice Notley (3)
Frank O'Hara (12)
Michael Ondaatje (3)
Ovid (4)
Nicanor Parra (4)
Cesare Pavese (3)
Sylvia Plath (8)
Edgar Allen Poe (3)
Ezra Pound (8)
Rainer Maria Rilke (9)
Arthur Rimbaud (3)
Theodore Roethke (3)
William Shakespeare (11)
Percy Shelley (3)
Ron Silliman (3)
Charles Simic (6)
Jack Spicer (4)
William Stafford (4)
Wallace Stevens (10)
Gertrude Stein (4)
May Swenson (3)
James Tate (5)
Dylan Thomas (4)
Henry David Thoreau (6)
Mark Twain (4)
César Vallejo (5)
Virgil (3)
Simone Weil (3)
Walt Whitman (16)
William Carlos Williams (17)
James Wright (7)
William Butler Yeats (11)

FREQUENTLY MENTIONED BOOKS:

The Bible, or some portion of it.
The Random House of Book of Twentieth Century French Poetry, ed. Paul Auster.
The New American Poetry, ed. Donald Allen.

CONTRIBUTORS

Ai writes, "I was born in Texas in 1947 to a family of Scot-Irish, Indian and Mulatto people and my father was Japanese. I am now working on a memoir about that. I am a full professor at Oklahoma State University and I live in Stillwater, Oklahoma, with five naughty cats." She has published seven books of poetry, including *Vice* which won the 1999 National Book Award. Her latest book is *Dread* (2003).

Nin Andrews was born May 6, 1958 and is the author of several books of poetry, most recently *Any Kind of Excuse* (2003). She is also the author of three editions of *The Book of Orgasms* (each edition is unique), which have been published as fiction, "even though she would prefer to think of her orgasms as poetry." She is currently working on a manuscript, *Dick and Jane in Midlife Crisis*, which is being published in regular installments on *Web Del Sol*. A yogini, Andrews lives in Poland, Ohio with her physicist-husband and her little dog, too.

Antler was born in Wisconsin in 1946. In addition to his many books of poetry, his work has appeared in over 1000 magazines and 150 anthologies, including most recently, *Poets Against the War* (2003). When not wildernessing or traveling to perform his poetry, he lives near the Milwaukee River; he was chosen by Friends of Milwaukee Public Library to be Poet Laureate of Milwaukee during 2002-2003.

Rae Armantrout was born in Vallejo, California, in 1947. She has published eight books of poetry, most recently *Veil: New and Selected Poems* (2001). She is also the author of a prose memoir, *True* (1998). She is currently completing *Up To Speed*, a collection of poems, and an as yet untitled manuscript of collected prose. She teaches writing at the University of California, San Diego.

Angela Ball was born on July 6, 1952 and is Professor and Chair of English at the University of Southern Mississippi. Her poems have appeared in such journals as *Partisan Review*, *Ploughshares*, *The New Republic*, and *The New Yorker*. She is the author of four full-length collections of poetry, the most recent of which is *The Museum of the Revolution* (1999). Her work is widely anthologized, including in *The Best American Poetry 2001*.

Marvin Bell was born in New York City in 1937. The most recent of his seventeen books of poetry are *Rampant* (2004) and *Nightworks:*

Poems 1962-2000 (2003). Iowa's first Poet Laureate, he lives in Iowa City and Port Townsend, Washington, and leads an annual Urban Teachers Workshop for America, SCORES, collaborates with composers, musicians and dancers, and teaches a master class for the Rainier Writing Workshop MFA@PLU.

Charles Bernstein was born in New York City in 1950. He has published 27 collections of poetry including *The Sophist* (reprinted in 2004) and *With Strings* (2001). His essays are included in *Content's Dream: Essays 1975-1984* (reprinted in 2001) and *My Way: Speeches and Poems* (1999). Bernstein is Professor of English at the University of Pennsylvania, where he is the co-director of PennSound, a web audio archive of poetry readings. He met Susan Bee in 1968 and they have collaborated on many projects since that time, including Emma (born 1985) and Felix (born 1992).

Anselm Berrigan was born on August 14, 1972, in Chicago, Illinois but grew up in New York City. After spending seven years in Buffalo and San Francisco, he moved back to New York in 1996. He is the author of *Zero Star Hotel* (2002), *Integrity & Dramatic Life* (1999), and numerous chapbooks. Berrigan is the Artistic Director of The Poetry Project at St. Mark's Church, and has had his poetry translated into French, Catalan, Romanian, and Slovenian.

Eavan Boland was born in Dublin, Ireland, in 1944. Her most recent books of poetry are *Against Love Poems* (2001) and *The Lost Land* (1998). In addition to books of poetry, Boland is the author of *Object Lessons: The Life of the Woman and the Poet in Our Time* (1995), a volume of prose. She is a regular reviewer for the *Irish Times* and a professor of English at Stanford University.

Catherine Bowman was born in El Paso, Texas, in 1957. Her two collections of poetry are *Rock Farm* (1996) and *1-800-HOT-RIBS* (1993). She is regularly featured on National Public Radio's "All Things Considered," and is the editor of *Word of Mouth: Poems Featured on NPR's All Things Considered* (2003). She teaches at Indiana University.

Alan Catlin has published sixty books of poetry. His work has appeared in over 500 separate electronic and print publications and been honored by fifteen Pushcart nominations.

Henri Cole was born in Fukuoka, Japan in 1956. His most recent collection, *Middle Earth* (2003), won the 2004 Kingsley Tufts Poetry Award and was a finalist for the Pulitzer Prize.

Wanda Coleman was born in November 1946, in the South Los Angeles community of Watts. Because she was a working mother, unable to complete her formal education, Coleman's "warrior voice" is the product of several writing workshops and life-long independent study inspired by poet Henri Coulette, with whom she briefly studied. She has received a Guggenheim Fellowship, been a bronze-medal finalist for the National Book Award, worked as a columnist for *The Los Angeles Times Magazine*, and been an Emmy-winning scriptwriter. Her new books are *Wanda Coleman's Greatest Hits 1966-2003* (2004) and *The Riot Inside Me: More Trials & Tremors* (2004). She resides in Southern California with her husband, poet-painter Austin Straus, and family.

Clark Coolidge was born on February 26, 1939 in Providence, Rhode Island, where his father was a professor of music at Brown University. Since 1997, he has lived in San Francisco's North Bay (Petaluma). The author of over thirty books, he regularly performs jazz and poetry with David Meltzer. His new book, *The Act of Providence*, will be published in 2005.

Jim Daniels was born on June 6, 1956. His most recent books are *Show and Tell: New and Selected Poems* (2003) and a book of fiction, *Detroit Tales* (2003). He is the Thomas S. Baker Professor of English at Carnegie Mellon University where he directs the creative writing program. He lives in Pittsburgh with his wife, Kristin Kovacic, and their children, Ramsey and Rosalie.

Denise Duhamel was born in 1961 and teaches at Florida International University in Miami. Widely anthologized, her poems have appeared in *The Best American Poetry* (1993, 1994, 1998, and 2000). Her latest book of poetry is *Two and Two* (2005). She lives in Hollywood, on the beach, and loves to ride her bike in the boardwalk's bike lane.

Stephen Dunn was born June 24, 1939 in Forest Hills, New York. He is the author of two books of prose and twelve books of poetry, including *The Insistence of Beauty* (2004) and *Different Hours*, which won the 2001 Pulitzer Prize for poetry. He is Distinguished Professor of Creative Writing at Richard Stockton College. Presently, Dunn lives in

Frostburg, Maryland with his wife, the writer Barbara Hurd.

Russell Edson was born in 1935 and lives in Connecticut with his wife, Frances. The most recent of his many books are *O Túnel* (2002), *The House of Sara Loo* (2002), *The Tormented Mirror* (2000), *The Tunnel: Selected Poems* (1994), and a novel, *The Song of Percival Peacock* (1992).

Elaine Equi was born on July 24, 1953 in Oak Park, Illinois. Most recently she is the author of *The Cloud of Knowable Things* (2003), but she has published many other collections of poetry including *Voice-Over* (1999), which won the San Francisco State Poetry Award. Her work is widely anthologized and appears in P*ostmodern American Poetry: A Norton Anthology* and in *The Best American Poetry* (1989, 1995, and 2002.) She teaches creative writing in the graduate program at City College and in The New School's MFA Program. Currently she lives in Manhattan with her husband, poet Jerome Sala.

Clayton Eshleman was born in 1935. He has recently published *My Devotion* (2004) and *Juniper Fuse: Upper Paleolithic Imagination & the Construction of the Underworld* (2003). Retired from Eastern Michigan University in 2003, he continues to lead tours to the Ice Age painted caves of the French Dordogne with his wife, Caryl, and "to work on getting the grain of the American political atmosphere into a language that also lies out on the dragon's tongue."

B. H. Fairchild was born in Houston, Texas in 1942 and grew up there and in small towns in west Texas, Oklahoma, and southwest Kansas. He has worked part-time as a technical writer for a nitroglycerin plant and as an English tutor to the University of Kansas basketball team. His third book, *The Art of the Lathe* (1998), was a Finalist for the National Book Award and received numerous awards including the California Book Award. Fairchild's latest book of poems, *Early Occult Memory Systems of the Lower Midwest* (2002), has received the National Book Critics Circle Award, the Gold Medal in Poetry from the California Book Awards, and the Texas Institute of Letters Poetry Award. He currently lives in Claremont, California, fifteen minutes from the Santa Anita racetrack.

Annie Finch was born on October 31, 1956 in New Rochelle, New York. In 1963-64, she spent over a year camping in Greece and other countries. Her first book of poetry, *The Encyclopedia of Scotland,* was completed in 1982 and published in 2004. Her other books include *Eve* (1997) and *Calendars* (2003), as well as a translation of the complete poems of Louise Labé. Her book of essays, *The Body of Poetry*, is forthcoming in the Poets on Poetry series from University of Michigan Press. For most of her life, she has spent each summer in the Maine woods with no running water or electricity. She teaches creative writing at Miami University, Ohio.

Alice Friman was born on October 20, 1933 and is the author of seven collections of poetry, most recently *Zoo* (1999), winner of the Ezra Pound Poetry Award and the Sheila Margaret Motton Prize. *Shenandoah* awarded her the 2002 James Boatwright III Prize for Poetry. In 2001-02, Friman was named to the Georgia Poetry Circuit. Professor Emerita at the University of Indianapolis, she now makes her home in Milledgeville, Georgia, where she is Instructor of Creative Writing and Poetry, and Associate Editor of *Arts and Letters* (Georgia College & State University).

Amy Gerstler was born in 1956, the year that the soap operas "As the World Turns" and "Edge of Night" premiered. She is the author of a number of poetry books, including *Medicine* (2000), *Crown of Weeds* (1997), and *Bitter Angel*, which won the National Book Critics Circle Award in 1991. Her most recent book of poems is entitled *Ghost Girl* (2004). She currently has three dogs and is restraining herself (so far) from adopting more. She is also a card carrying member of the American Society for Psychical Research.

Albert Goldbarth was born in Chicago, Illinois in 1948. Two of his many poetry collections have received the National Book Critics Circle Award. He is also the author of four books of essays and a novel, *Pieces of Payne* (2003). His newest collection of poems is *Budget Travel Through Space and Time* (2005). He currently lives in Wichita, Kansas, without a computer (his fingers have never touched one), but with a lovely collection of 1950's space toys, mainly "rocketships and ray guns."

Gabriel Gudding was born in 1966. His first book of poems, *A Defense of Poetry*, was published in 2002. An assistant professor of literature and creative writing at Illinois State University, he is a recipient of such awards as The Nation Discovery Award, the Constance Saltonstall Artist's Grant, and the Starrett Prize. His poetry and short fiction appear in such venues as *The American Poetry Review*, *Seneca Review*, *The Nation*, and *Jacket*. He has initiated creative writing programs in prisons at Auburn, New York and Holly Springs, Mississippi.

Thom Gunn was born in England in 1929. He came to California in 1954 and studied with Yvor Winters during a one year fellowship at Stanford. He lived in San Francisco and taught at Berkeley for many years. He is the author of over thirty books of poetry, most recently *Boss Cupid* (2000), *Frontiers of Gossip* (1998), *Collected Poems* (1994), and *The Man with Night Sweats* (1992), which won the Lenore Marshall Poetry Prize. Thom Gunn died on April 25, 2004 at his home in San Francisco.

Sam Hamill was born in 1943, orphaned, and adopted by a Utah farm family. He came to poetry and to Zen as a teenager, became a Conscientious Objector while serving in the U. S. Marine Corps, and ran for California state assembly in 1968. He taught in prisons for 14 years and has worked extensively with battered women and children. He is co-founder and Artistic Director at Copper Canyon Press, founder of *Poets Against the War*, and the author of 40-odd books, including translations from classical Chinese, Japanese, Greek, Latin, and Estonian. His newest book, *Almost Paradise: Selected Poems & Translations*, will be published in March, 2005.

Joy Harjo, born in Tulsa, Oklahoma, in 1951, is a poet, musician, writer, and performer. She has published many books including, most recently, *How We Became Human, New and Selected Poems* (2002) and her first children's book, *The Good Luck Cat* (2000). She is a saxophone player and performs nationally and internationally, solo and with a band. Her newest music project is *Native Joy for Real*. She is a member of the Muscogee Nation, a member of the Tallahassee Wakokaye Grounds, and a professor at UCLA. She lives in Honolulu.

Michael S. Harper was born in Brooklyn, New York, in 1938. He has published more than ten books of poetry, including *Songlines* in *Michaeltree: New and Collected Poems* (2000), *Honorable Amendments* (1995), and *Images of Kin* (1977), which won the Melville-Cane Award from the Poetry Society of America and was nominated for the National Book Award. He is the co-editor of *The Vintage Book of African American Poetry* (2000) and he served as the first Poet Laureate of the State of Rhode Island, 1988-1993. Harper is University Professor and Professor of English at Brown University, where he has taught since 1970.

Lola Haskins was born in 1943 and is the author of seven books of poetry, most recently *Desire Lines: New and Selected Poems* (2004) and *The Rim Benders* (2001). Her awards include the Emily Dickinson/Writer Magazine award from the Poetry Society of America. She has collaborated often with other artists. For instance, she performed her book, *Forty-Four Ambitions for the Piano* (1990), with Kevin Sharpe, a classical pianist and James Paul Sain, an electronic composer, and she played "the speaking Mata Hari" in a ballet of that title, for which she wrote the libretto. As a day job, she teaches Computer Science at the University of Florida.

Bob Hicok was born in 1960. His latest book is *Insomnia Diary* (2004). His previous book, *Animal Soul* (2001), was a finalist for the National Book Critics Circle Award. *The Legend of Light* won the 1995 Felix Pollak Prize from Wisconsin and was an ALA Notable Book of the Year. He started teaching in 2003 at Virginia Tech after working for 20 years designing automotive dies. At 44, he "became a fan of the seven ounce beer."

Tony Hoagland, born in 1953, has published three collections of poetry, most recently, *What Narcissism Means To Me* (2003), nominated for the National Book Critics Circle Award. His collection *Donkey Gospel* won 1998 James Laughlin Award. He has received four Pushcart Prizes and twice been included in *The Best American Poetry* anthology series. He currently teaches in the graduate writing program of the University of Houston and in the Warren Wilson MFA program. A book of prose about poetry, *Real Sofistikashun*, is forthcoming.

Paul Hoover was born in Virginia in 1946. He lived for many years in Chicago before moving to San Francisco to serve as Visiting Professor of Creative Writing at San Francisco State University. He is married to the fiction writer and poet Maxine Chernoff, with whom he edits the literary magazine *New American Writing*. He has published eight poetry collections, including *Winter (Mirror)* (2002) and *Rehearsal in Black* (2001). His collection of literary essays, *Fables of Representation* was published in the Poets on Poetry series of University of Michigan Press in 2004. He is also editor of the anthology *Postmodern American Poetry* (1994).

Fanny Howe writes, "I was born in 1940, grew up in Massachusetts and headed west when I was 17 to study at Stanford. I have three grown children and three grandchildren. For many years I taught at UCSD. Recently I taught at The New School. My publications include *The*

Wedding Dress (2003), *Selected Poems* (2000) and *Gone* (2003), all from UC Press, several short novels from Sun and Moon Books, and a novel called *Indivisible* (2000) from Semiotexte."

Andrew Hudgins was born in Killeen, Texas in 1951. He is the author of six books of poetry, the latest of which is *Ecstatic in the Poison* (2003) and one book of criticism, *The Glass Anvil* (1997) which is part of the University of Michigan's Poets on Poetry series. He teaches in the MFA program at Ohio State University.

Lisa Jarnot was born in Buffalo, New York on November 26, 1967. She studied at the State University of New York at Buffalo and at Brown University, receiving a MFA degree in 1994. She is the author of three full-length collections of poetry: *Black Dog Songs* (2003), *Ring of Fire* (2001), and *Some Other Kind of Mission* (1996). Jarnot has worked as a librarian, a pizza maker, a dish washer, and a teacher. She currently teaches in the MFA programs at Brooklyn College and at Naropa University. She lives in Brooklyn, New York.

Peter Johnson was born February 22, 1951. His latest book of prose poems, *Miracles & Mortifications*, received the 2001 James Laughlin Award from The Academy of American Poets. He has received creative writing fellowships from the NEA in 1999 and the Rhode Island Council on the Arts in 2002. His new book of prose poems, *Eduardo and "I"*, will be published by White Pine Press in 2006. He lives in Providence, Rhode Island with his wife and two sons.

X. J. Kennedy was born in 1929 in Dover, New Jersey. He is a veteran of four years as a journalist in the U. S. Navy's Atlantic Fleet, a winner of the Los Angeles Times Book Prize, and the former poetry editor of *The Paris Review*. Presently, he lives in Lexington, Massachusetts, where he reads to six small grandchildren out of some of his twenty books for children. In 2004, *The Lords of Misrule: Poems 1992-2001* received the Poets' Prize.

David Kirby was born on November 29, 1944. He is the author of numerous books of poetry and criticism, including an essay collection entitled *What Is a Book?* (2002). His poetry collection *The House of Blue Light* (2000) was selected by Dave Smith as part of the Southern Messenger Poets Series published by Louisiana State University Press. *The Ha-Ha* (2003), his most recent book, appeared under the same imprint. He is married to the poet Barbara Hamby. When they are not writing, David and Barbara "like to dine well and travel far."

Maxine Kumin was born in Philadelphia in 1925. She is the author of thirteen books of poetry, most recently *The Long Marriage* (2003) and *Bringing Together: Uncollected Early Poems 1958-1988* (2003) as well as a memoir, *Inside the Halo: Anatomy of a Recovery* (2002). She won the Pulitzer Prize in Poetry in 1973 and has subsequently been awarded the Aiken Taylor Prize, the Poets' Prize, the Harvard Graduate School of Arts and Sciences Centennial Award, and the Ruth E. Lilly Prize, among others. In 1980-81, she served as Consultant in Poetry to the Library of Congress, a post now known as Poet Laureate. She and her husband live on a farm in New Hampshire.

David Lehman was born in New York City in 1948. Like Ben Jonson, William Styron, Irving Howe, and Josephine Miles, he was born on June 11. Lehman wrote his first poems in high school. Both were entitled "Ode," and both were four lines long. The first:

> I asked a fat man,
> Do you enjoy being fat?
> Yes, he said,
> That is the only thing that I enjoy.

The second:

> As long as I live,
> there shall never be
> another Harry
> > S. Truman.

He went to Columbia, then to Cambridge University on a Kellett Fellowship. Returning to Columbia in 1972, he worked for a year as Lionel Trilling's research assistant. In 1978 Lehman completed his dissertation—on the prose poem in England and America—and received his doctorate. He says that the best professional decision he ever made was to leave academe and to earn his living as a free-lance writer. This he did in 1982. His books of poetry include *The Evening Sun* (2002) and *The Daily Mirror* (2000). He has also written such nonfiction books as *The Perfect Murder: A Study in Detection* (2000) and *Signs of the Times: Deconstruction and the Fall of Paul de Man* (1991). He is the series editor of *The Best American Poetry*, which he initiated in 1988.

Phillip Levine was born in Detroit in 1928. He divides his time between Fresno, California and Brooklyn, New York. His awards include two National Book Awards and one Pulitzer. In 2004, Knopf published his 17ᵗʰ collection of poetry, *Breath*.

Lyn Lifshin's most recent book of poetry is *Another Woman Who Looks Like Me* (2004). Also recently published is *A New Film by a Woman in Love with the Dead* (2002). She has published more than 100 books of poetry and edited four anthologies of women's writing. She is the subject of an award winning documentary film, *Lyn Lifshin: Not Made of Glass*. Lifshin writes, "Besides poetry, one other obsession is ballet–I take about 7 or 8 classes a week. I love Abyssinian cats and, recently, became obsessed with a gorgeous and tragic supernatural race horse, Ruffian (whom I am working on a collection of poems about). I've become fascinated with horse racing, just the beauty and danger and ambivalence, not the betting."

Timothy Liu was born in San Jose, California in 1965. His first book of poems, *Vox Angelica*, received the 1992 Norma Farber First Book Award from the Poetry Society of America. His most recent books are *Of Thee I Sing* (2004) and *Hard Evidence* (2001). He is also the editor of *Word of Mouth: An Anthology of Gay American Poetry* (2000). An associate Professor of English at William Paterson University, Liu makes his home in Hoboken, New Jersey.

Gerald Locklin was born in Rochester, New York, in 1941. He is professor emeritus at California State University, Long Beach. His books and chapbooks of poetry and fiction number over 125, including, most recently, *The Pocket Book: A Novella and Nineteen Short Fictions* (2003) and *The Life Force Poems* (2002). His work is archived by CSU Long Beach Special Collections and indexed on their website. He enjoys jazz, art, opera, travel, Diet Pepsi, the Lakers, the Yankees, and *The Sopranos*. He does not enjoy swimming but does it anyway to stay alive. So far he can still leave the floor when performing his "Tap Dancing" note at readings, but, he adds, "you never know when you may be doing your last 'Bell Step'."

Thomas Lux was born in Northampton, Massachusetts, in 1946. His numerous books of poetry include *The Cradle Place* (2004), *The Street of Clocks* (2001), and *New and Selected Poems, 1975-1995* (1997), which was a finalist for the 1998 Lenore Marshall Poetry Prize. He has won three National Endowment for the Arts grants and a Guggenheim Fellowship. Currently he teaches at Georgia Tech University.

J. D. McClatchy was born in Bryn Mawr, Pennsylvania, in 1945. He is the author of five books of poetry including, *Hazmat* (2002) and *Ten Commandments* (1998). He has also published two collections of essays: *Twenty Questions* (1998) and *White Paper* (1989). He has written four opera libretti, most recently *Emmeline* for Tobias Picker, commissioned by the Santa Fe Opera. Since 1991 he has been editor of *The Yale Review*. From 1996 to 2003, McClatchy served as a Chancellor of The Academy of American Poets. He lives in Stonington, Connecticut. His latest book is *American Writers at Home* (2004).

Peter Meinke was born December 29, 1932. He has published twelve books of poetry, most recently *Zinc Fingers*, which received the 2001 SEBA Award from the Southeast Booksellers Association. His poems have also received the Paumanok Award, the Emily Dickinson Award, and the Sow's Ear Chapbook Prize. His collection of stories, *The Piano Tuner*, was given the 1986 Flannery O'Connor Award. He has recently been appointed to the Darden Chair in Creative Writing at Old Dominion University in Norfolk, Virginia.

E. Ethelbert Miller was born November 20, 1950. He is the former chair of the Humanities Council of Washington, D. C. and is a core faculty member of the Bennington Writing Seminars at Bennington College. He has been the director of the African American Resource Center at Howard University since 1974. His most recent book of poetry is *How We Sleep on the Nights We Don't Make Love* (2004). His memoir *Fathering Words: The Making of an African American Writer* (2000) was selected by the DC WE READ program in 2003 as the book all Washington residents were encouraged to read. He has twice been honored by Laura Bush and the White House at the National Book Festival. His poetry has been heard on the HBO Def Jam Poetry program and he can regularly be heard on National Public Radio.

Thylias Moss was born in Cleveland, Ohio, in 1954. Her most recent book of poetry is *Slave Moth: A Narrative in Verse* (2004). She is the author of a memoir, *Tale of a Sky-Blue Dress* (1998), and two plays. Among her honors are a MacArthur Fellowship, a Guggenheim Fellowship, and a Dewar's Profiles Performance Award. She is a professor of English at the University of Michigan and lives in Ann Arbor with her husband and two sons.

Naomi Shihab Nye was born in 1952 and was a Lannan Fellow in 2003. Her recent books include *19 Varieties of Gazelle: Poems of the Middle East* (2002) and *Come with Me* (2000), which was a finalist for the

National Book Award. Her book *Habibi* (1999) is a novel for teens and she has edited seven prize-winning anthologies of poetry for young readers, including *What Have You Lost?* (2001) and *Salting the Ocean* (2000).

Ed Ochester was born in Brooklyn in 1939. His most recent books are *The Land of Cockaigne* (2001) and *Snow White Horses: Selected Poems* (2000). He edits the Pitt Poetry Series, is general editor of the Drue Heinz Literature Prize for short fiction, and is a member of the core faculty at the Bennington MFA Program. He has twice been elected president of Associated Writing Programs and for many years was director of the Writing Program at the University of Pittsburgh. He and his wife Britt live in a rural county northeast of Pittsburgh where they raise multitudinous flowers and feed innumerable birds. With Judith Vollmer he edits the poetry magazine *5 AM*. He passed through Cornell, Harvard and the University of Wisconsin, and has never quite gotten over the '60s.

Molly Peacock, born in 1947, Poet-in-Residence at The American Poets' Corner, Cathedral of St. John the Divine, and former President of The Poetry Society of America, is the author of five volumes of poetry, including *Cornucopia: New & Selected Poems* (2002). She also performs a one-woman show in poems, *The Shimmering Verge*, and is the author of a memoir, *Paradise, Piece by Piece* (1998). She lives in Toronto and New York City with her husband, the James Joyce scholar Michael Groden. She has a balcony garden in summer, a few orchids in winter, and cats all year round.

Lucia Perillo has published three books of poetry. Her poetry, essays and short fiction have appeared in many magazines and have been reprinted in the *Pushcart* and *The Best American Poetry* anthologies. In 2000, she received a MacArthur Foundation fellowship. Her new book, *Luck is Luck*, is forthcoming in 2005. She lives in Olympia, Washington.

Carl Phillips, born in 1959, grew up on air force bases all over the U. S. and in Germany, before settling in Massachusetts, where he studied Classics at Harvard and taught high school Latin for ten years. Phillips is the author of seven books of poems, most recently *The Rest of Love* (2004) and *Rock Harbor* (2002); other books include *Coin of the Realm: Essays on the Life and Art of Poetry* (2004) and a translation of Sophocles' *Philoctetes* (2003). His awards and honors include the

Kingsley Tufts Poetry Award and fellowships from the Guggenheim Foundation and the Library of Congress. He divides his time between Cape Cod, Massachusetts and St. Louis, Missouri, where he is Professor of English at Washington University.

Robert Pinsky was born in Long Branch, New Jersey, in 1940. He is the author of six books of poetry, most recently *Jersey Rain* (2000). He has also published four books of criticism, including *The Sounds of Poetry* (1998), which was a finalist for the National Book Critics Circle Award. In 1997, Pinsky was named the United States Poet Laureate and Consultant in Poetry to the Library of Congress. During his unprecedented three-year tenure, he initiated the Favorite Poem Project which documents, by video, individual Americans discussing their favorite poems. Currently he is the poetry editor of the weekly internet magazine, *Slate*, and teaches in the graduate writing program at Boston University. He recently completed a book of prose on King David.

Charles Potts was born in Idaho, in 1943 and has been a resident of Walla Walla, Washington since 1978, where he operates The Temple Bookstore and School of Poetry, www.thetemplebookstore.com. He has published two literary periodicals, *Litmus* (in the '60s and '70s) and *The Temple* (in the '90s and '00s). He has eleven books in print including, *Campostrella/Starfield* (2004), *Across the North Pacific* (2002), and *Slash & Burn* (2001).

Donald Revell was born in The Bronx, New York in June of 1954. He is the author of eight collections of poetry, most recently, *My Mojave* (2003) and *Arcady* (2002). He is also the translator of two volumes of the poetry of Guillaume Apollinaire, *The Self-Dismembered Man* (2004) and *Alcools* (1995). Revell writes, "Presently, I am a Professor of English and Director of Creative Writing Programs at the University of Utah. Together with my wife, poet Claudia Keelan, and our son, Benjamin, I live on a half-acre of lizards, verbena, and locust trees in Arden, Nevada."

Adrienne Rich was born in Baltimore in 1929. W. H. Auden selected her first book as winner of the Yale Younger Poets Prize in 1951. Her latest volume of poetry is *The School Among the Ruins: Poems 2000-2004* (2004). She edited Muriel Rukeyser's *Selected Poems* for the Library of America and has received many awards, including the Ruth Lilly Prize, the Wallace Stevens Award, a MacArthur Fellowship, and the Bollingen Prize. Rich has three sons and two grandchildren and has lived for nearly thirty years with the writer Michelle Cliff.

Harvey Shapiro was born in 1924 and is the author of ten books of poetry, the most recent of which is *How Charlie Shavers Died* (2001). Carcanet Press in England and Wesleyan co-published his *Selected Poems* in 1997. He recently edited the anthology *Poets of World War II* (2003) for the Library of America. He worked as an editor of *The New York Times Magazine* for many years and from 1975-83 was the editor of *The New York Times Book Review*. He has two sons and three grand-children.

Ron Silliman was born in 1946 and, once upon a time, attended UC Berkeley and San Francisco State. He has written and edited 25 books to date, most recently *Woundwood* (2004). In 2004, he finished writing "The Alphabet," a long poem he began in 1979. He was a 2003 Literary Fellow of the National Endowment for the Arts and a 2002 Fellow of the Pennsylvania Arts Council as well as a Pew Fellow in the Arts in 1998. He lives in Chester County, Pennsylvania, with his wife and two sons, and works as a market analyst in the computer industry.

W. D. Snodgrass, born in Pennsylvania in 1926, is a Distinguished Professor Emeritus at the University of Delaware. He has received awards from the Academy of American Poets, the National Institute of Arts and Letters, and the National Endowment for the Arts. His first book, *Heart's Needle*, won the Pulitzer for Poetry in 1960. Subsequently, Snodgrass has published many books of poetry and trans-lations. Recently, he published two books of criticism, *To Sound Like Yourself* (2003) and *De/Compositions: 101 Good Poems Gone Wrong* (2001). He lives with his wife, the critic and translator, Kathleen Snodgrass, in Erieville, New York and San Miguel de Allende, Mexico.

Juliana Spahr was born in Chillicothe, Ohio in 1966. Her books include *Fuck You-Aloha-I Love You* (2001), *Everybody's Autonomy: Connective Reading and Collective Identity* (2001), and *Response* (1996). She co-edits the journal *Chain* with Jena Osman. She frequently self-pub-lishes her work.

Elizabeth Spires was born in 1952. She is the author of five collections of poetry, most recently *Now the Green Blade Rises* (2002). She is also the author of five children's books, including *The Mouse of Amherst* (1999) which is the story of a small mouse inspired to write poetry after moving into Emily Dickinson's bedroom. *Publisher's Weekly* cited it as a "Best Book of 1999." Her free lance reviews of children's books appear in *The New York Times*. She lives in Baltimore with her husband, the novelist Madison Smartt Bell, and their daughter Celia, and teaches poetry at Goucher College, where she holds a Chair for Distinguished Achievement.

David St. John, born in Fresno, California on July 24, 1949, has received numerous awards for his poetry, including an Award in Literature from the American Academy and Institute of Arts and Letters. His most recent book is *The Face* (2004). He lives in Venice, California and is the Director of the Ph. D. Program in Literature and Creative Writing at the University of Southern California. He was raised to be a tennis player and is a mediocre, but enthusiastic, guitarist.

Gerald Stern was born in Pittsburgh, Pennsylvania in 1925, the son of immigrant Polish and Ukrainian Jews. He is the author of thirteen books of poetry, including *This Time, New and Selected Poems*, which won the National Book Award in 1998, and a book of personal essays, *What I Can't Bear Losing*, which was published in 2003. He has spent much of his life on the Delaware River that separates New Jersey and Pennsylvania and claims both of these states as his own.

Virgil Suárez was born in Havana, Cuba in 1962. Since 1974, he has lived in the United States. He is the author of over twenty books of prose and poetry, most recently *Infinite Refuge* (2002) and *Guide to the Blue Tongue* (2002). His poem "La Florida" appears in the *The Best American Poetry 2004*. In the winter of 2005, the University of Pittsburgh Press will publish *90 Miles: Selected and New Poems*. He is the co-editor of four anthologies published by the University of Iowa Press. Currently, he is writing a novel and restoring a '55 Chevrolet.

David Trinidad was born in 1953 in southern California. His most recent book, *Phoebe 2002: An Essay in Verse* (2003), is a mock-epic based on the 1950 film *All About Eve*, co-written with Jeffery Conway and Lynn Crosbieit. His other books include *Plasticville* (2000) and *Answer Song* (1994). He is a Poet-in-Residence at Columbia College in Chicago, where he also coordinates the Graduate Poetry Program.

Paul Violi was born in New York in 1944. His books of poems include *Breakers* (2000) and *Fracas* (1998). Hanging Loose Press recently published his book of short non-fiction, *Selected Accidents, Pointless Anecdotes* (2002). In 2001 he received the Zabel Award from the

American Academy of Arts and Letters. He is also the recipient of the John Ciardi Lifetime Achievement Award and two poetry fellowships from the NEA. He teaches Imaginative Writing at Columbia University as well as courses at NYU and in the graduate writing program at the New School University.

Karen Volkman was born in 1967. Her books of poetry are *Crash's Law* (1996) and *Spar*, which received the Iowa Poetry Prize and the 2002 James Laughlin Award from the Academy of American Poets. Her poems, essays, and reviews have appeared in numerous journals and anthologies. Recipient of awards and fellowships from the National Endowment for the Arts and the Poetry Society of America, she currently teaches in the MFA program at the University of Montana.

David Wagoner was born in Massillon, Ohio in 1926. He has published seventeen books of poems, most recently *The House of Song* (2002), and ten novels, one of which, *The Escape Artist*, was made into a movie by Francis Ford Coppola. Wagoner won the Lilly Prize in 1991, and has been nominated twice for the National Book Award. He was a chancellor of the Academy of American Poets for 23 years. He has taught at the University of Washington since 1954 and was the editor of *Poetry Northwest* until its end in 2002. His new book, *Good Morning and Good Night* will be published in 2005.

Charles Harper Webb's most recent book of poetry is *Tulip Farms and Leper Colonies* (2001). His book *Reading the Water* won the 1997 S. F. Morse Poetry Prize and the 1998 Kate Tufts Discovery Award. *Liver* won the 1999 Felix Pollak Prize. He is the editor of *Stand Up Poetry: An Expanded Anthology* (2002) and co-editor of *Grand Passion: The Poets of Los Angeles*. For many years, he was a professional singer-guitarist.

Dara Wier has published eight books including *Hat on a Pond* (2001) and *Voyages in English* (2001). She teaches at the University of Massachusetts. Guggenheim, NEA and Massachusetts Cultural Council fellowships have supported her work. Selections of her poems have been awarded the Jerome Shestack Prize by the *American Poetry Review* and her work has been included in *The Best American Poetry* and *The Pushcart Prize* anthologies. Born in New Orleans, she grew up on a farm and citrus orchard south of the city down near the mouth of the Mississippi; this accounts for her fondness for mules and rivers, and all things Creole.

Richard Wilbur was born in 1921, in New York City, and grew up on a farm in New Jersey. He went to Amherst, served overseas with the 36th Division in World War II, and returned to become a teacher of English and Humanities at Harvard, Wellesley, Wesleyan, and Smith, retiring in 1986. He has written criticism, show lyrics (*Candide*), and children's books; his translations of Molière and Racine are widely performed; and his poems, honored recently by the Wallace Stevens Award, are gathered in *Collected Poems 1943-2004* (2004). Wilbur and his wife Charlotte have four children and three grandchildren, and live in Cummington, Massachusetts and Key West.

C. K. Williams, born in New Jersey in 1936, is the author of nine books of poetry, the most recent of which, *The Singing*, won the National Book Award in 2003. *Repair* was awarded the 2000 Pulitzer Prize, and his *Flesh and Blood* (1987) received the National Book Critics Circle Award. He has published translations of Sophocles' *Women of Trachis* (1992), Euripides' *Bacchae* (1990), and poems of Francis Ponge, among others. His book of essays, *Poetry and Consciousness*, appeared in 1998, and a memoir, *Misgivings*, in 2000. He teaches in the Writing Program at Princeton University, and lives part of the year in the country in France.

C. D. Wright was born in 1949 in Mountain Home, Arkansas. Among her many honors, she was named State Poet of Rhode Island in 1994, a five-year post. She writes, "I live in Rhode Island with poet Forrest Gander, son Brecht, greyhound Jackie. Most recent book is *One Big Self: Prisoners* of Louisiana, photographs by Deborah Luster (the text is mine). Next book is prose, *Cooling Time: An American Poetry Vigil*."

Charles Wright, winner of a Pulitzer Prize, the Los Angeles Book Prize, and a National Book Award, writes, "I was born on 25 August 1935, in Pickwick Dam, Tenn. I spent my first 21 years in Appalachia. The rest of my life primarily in Italy, California, and Virginia. Currently I live in Charlottesville, VA, and spend the summers in northwest Montana. My latest book is *Buffalo Yoga* (2004)."

Franz Wright was born in Vienna in 1953. His most recent collections are *Walking to Martha's Vineyard*, which won the Pulitzer Prize in 2004, and *The Beforelife*, which was a finalist for the Pulitzer Prize in 2002. He is a recipient of the PEN/Voelcker Prize, as well as Guggenheim, Whiting, and NEA Fellowships. He works at the Edinburg Center for Mental Health and The Center for Grieving Children, and lives in

Waltham, Massachusetts with his wife, translator and writer, Elizabeth Oehlkers Wright. During the spring semester of 2004 he taught a graduate poetry workshop at the University of Arkansas, Fayetteville.

Dean Young has published five books of poems. His sixth, *Elegy on Toy Piano*, will be out from Pittsburg University Press in 2005. He teaches at the Iowa Writer's Workshop and in the Warren Wilson low-residency MFA program. He has only sky-dived twice, far fewer times than he pretends.

Paul Zimmer was born in 1934. Over the past thirty-five years, he has read his poems at more than 300 colleges and poetry centers. He has recorded his poems for the Library of Congress, and was twice awarded Writing Fellowships from the National Endowment for the Arts. He has published eight books of poetry, including *The Great Bird of Love* (1989), which was selected by William Stafford for the National Poetry Series. A new book of autobiographical essays is *Trains in the Distance* (2004). He worked as a scholarly publisher for thirty years and was founding editor of three ongoing poetry book series at Pitt, Georgia, and Iowa. He now lives on a farm in southwestern Wisconsin and part of each year in a small house in the south of France.

ACKNOWLEDGEMENTS CONTINUED.

"In A Station of the Metro." By Ezra Pound, from PERSONAE, copyright © 1926 by Ezra Pound. Reprinted by permission of New Directions Publishing Corp.

"In My Craft of Sullen Art." By Dylan Thomas, from THE POEMS OF DYLAN THOMAS, copyright © 1946 by New Directions Publishing Corp. Reprinted by permission of New Directions Publishing Corp.

"It Was Beginning Winter," from COLLECTED POEMS OF THEODORE ROETHKE by Theodore Roethke, copyright. Used by permission of Doubleday, a division of Random House, Inc.

James Wright, excerpts from "Two Hangovers" and "Stages on a Journey Westward " in THE BRANCH WILL NOT BREAK © 1963 by James Wright and reprinted by permission of Wesleyan University Press.

"Lament for Ignacio Sánchez Mejías." By Federico Garcia Lorca, Translated by Stephen Spender & J. L. Gili, from THE SELECTED POEMS OF FEDERICO GARCIA LORCA, copyright © 1955 by New Directions Publishing Corp. Reprinted by permission of New Directions Publishing Corp.

"The Moon Rising." By Federico García Lorca, Translated by Lysander Kemp, from THE SELECTED POEMS OF FEDERICO GARCIA LORCA, copyright © 1955 by New Directions Publishing Corp. Reprinted by permission of New Directions Publishing Corp.

"The Potter." By Pablo Neruda, from THE CAPTAIN'S VERSES, copyright © 1972 by Pablo Neruda and Donald D. Walsh. Reprinted by permission of New Directions Publishing Corp.

"Simplicity." By Henri Michaux, Translated by Sylvia Beach, from SELECTED WRITINGS, copyright © 1968 by New Directions Publishing Corp. Reprinted by permission of New Directions Publishing Corp.

Peter Davis is a poet and painter. He holds a MFA from Bennington College and he teaches at Ball State University. Some of his poems may be read at barnwoodpress.org, and a selection of his paintings may be seen at artisnecessary.com.With his wife, Jenny, and his son, Maxwell, he lives in Muncie, Indiana.